Our Boys Speak

JOHN NIKKAH
with Leah Furman

Adolescent Boys Write About
Their Inner Lives

ST. MARTIN'S GRIFFIN ☙ NEW YORK

www.stmartins.com

Book design by Kate Nichols

Library of Congress Cataloging-in-Publication Data

Nikkah, John.
   Our boys speak : adolescent boys write about their inner lives / John Nikkah. — 1st ed.
      p. cm.
   ISBN 0-312-26280-9 (pbk.)
   1. Teenage boys—United States—Psychology. 2. Teenagers' writings, American. I. Title.

HQ797.N55 2000
305.235—dc21

00-026415

First Edition: June 2000

10   9   8   7   6   5   4   3   2   1

For Mom and Dad

Contents

Acknowledgments

This book could not have been written without the foresight and dedication of my editor, Joe Veltre. Another person whose help and commitment I couldn't have done without is Leah Furman, who worked alongside me from beginning to end. I would also like to thank my agent, Giles Anderson, for having faith in my ability to get the job done. Mira Furman and Elina Furman should also be credited for lending a helping hand with the mailings and transcriptions. Their help was invaluable.

I would also like to thank my friends Mitch Rovner and Bobby Piñero, whose advice I could always count on, and especially my parents, whose support throughout my life has helped me achieve things I never thought possible.

Finally, I would like to thank all of the boys who contributed to the book, and the teachers who took time out of their busy schedules to encourage their students to express themselves.

Introduction
At War with Ourselves

WHEN I FIRST approached publishers in New York City about writing a book from the boys' point of view, many of them were reluctant and unconvinced that it would work. "Boys are not that open," they said. "We don't think boys can write on that level," they said. "We'd need to see the letters to believe it," they said. At first, I was taken aback by their response. After all, hadn't hundreds of girls bared their souls for the book *Ophelia Speaks*? Why wouldn't young boys be able to do the same?

Frustrated and confused, I began losing faith in the project.

Maybe they're right, I thought. After all, boys are not encouraged to speak out on behalf of their feelings. Much like I was raised, most boys are brought up to keep their emotions bottled up. Maybe we really are unable to achieve the same level of self-disclosure as our female counterparts.

Girl Power had become a sort of buzzword in the media. Everyone from societal pundits to celebrities was concerned with preaching the good word of female empowerment and strength. Just look at the number of magazines geared toward young girls as opposed to the number of magazines geared to solving boys' problems.

Girls, we were instructed, are extremely complicated and require special attention in order to counteract the many pressures exerted upon them. Boys, on the other hand, are made of a much tougher fiber and able to take care of themselves. Although I was quick to see the merit of espousing Girl Power to young, impressionable girls, I still couldn't help feeling that boys were in dire need of their own special brand of empowerment.

I resolved not to give up on my fellow man. Despite all of the criticism and skepticism that was heaped upon my project, my gut instinct told me that boys had a story to tell. And aren't their experiences, fears, and goals just as important as those of girls?

Just as I received what seemed to be my umpteenth rejection and felt my motivation was beginning to flag, an editor from St. Martin's Press came to the rescue. He also believed that boys were in dire need of a voice, and set me to the task of collecting letters from boys all over the country. Instead of coming up with a million reasons for why the book wouldn't work, he had faith that boys would come out in droves to support their own cause. Man, was I relieved. For a minute there, I'd thought I was the only one who was interested in championing the plight of boys and helping them express their views.

Spurred on by my editor's enthusiasm, I began the long process of collecting stories, poems, and journal entries from boys aged twelve to eighteen. With every stamp I pasted and every envelope I sealed (there were more than five thousand), my confidence and anticipation mounted. I couldn't help wondering how many boys would write, and what their tales would reveal. I actually became a little worried about what I would discover along the way. Like a cave explorer with only a small light to guide his way, I grew apprehensive about what I would find at the end of the tunnel.

You see, like everyone else, I, too, had been saddled with my share of stereotypes about boys. Boys, I thought, were more aggressive than girls. Boys didn't care about much, except fulfilling their sex drives. Boys didn't complain about their problems. And most of all, boys didn't feel life's disappointments as keenly as girls. I had grown up with these misconceptions, but as I matured and came in touch with my own feelings and emotions, I began to suspect that I had sold myself and my male peers short.

I've often heard it said that girls are much more difficult to raise than boys. To bring up a healthy young man, a parent need only leave him to his own devices, and hope he turns out to be a productive member of society. Of course, the idea that boys somehow need less attention has backfired, and parents and educators are only now beginning to understand the adverse effects of not paying attention to our boys.

Left to fend for themselves and to learn many of life's lessons from peripheral sources such as friends and television, many of our boys don't have the chance to develop mature and healthy outlooks on life. The recent outbreaks of violence in Littleton, Jonesboro, and a spate of other Middle American communities across the country show that boys are suffering from too many pressures, not enough attention, and an inability to find the very modes of expression that so many girls take for granted.

Knowing what I did about society's and my own misconceptions about boys, I hoped that the letters I received would somehow dispel my delusions. I wanted the letters to make an important statement about growing up male in this country. But what I got was so much more.

After poring over one letter after another, I could see that no matter how much credit I gave the young men growing up today, it had only been a small fraction of the respect and consideration that they actually deserve. Until I read their often poignant and painful admissions, I never knew just how difficult life had become for our youth. For me, high school had been a nice place to visit. I could meet my friends, talk to my girlfriend, and then cruise over to a local restaurant during lunch with some of my best buds. Pep rallies, sports games, parties, and school hangouts are what come to mind when I think back to school. My biggest problem at the time was figuring out how to better my grades so I could get into a good college.

But as I read the letters, I discovered just how sheltered my life had been. One boy likened the experience of returning from school to returning from a war. And on April 20, 1999, that particular analogy took on more meaning than the students of Columbine High School could ever have imagined.

As I watched the horrific footage from the Columbine tragedy, my feelings of shock and concern were also mingled with an overwhelming sense of gratitude, a gratitude for the fact that I had grown up in a time far removed from all the madness. Although I didn't graduate from high school until the early nineties, the marked lack of weapons, metal detectors, and mandatory mesh backpacks makes that time seem like a full generation ago. Looking at the shell-shocked faces of the Columbine students as they stumbled out of their worst nightmare gave me an uncomfortable sense of relief. I felt as if I had narrowly missed the chaos and terror that permeate the lives of students today. Instead of thinking about those students who did not survive the fatal shoot-out of that morning, I couldn't help but focus on the faces of the students running out of that now-dreadful building. I could identify with them, because I, too, had escaped just in the nick of time.

Or had I? Thinking about the Columbine tragedy and its victims, I began to realize that I, along with millions of boys who had survived adolescence, had not made it out without one or two battle scars of our own. I, too, was bruised and beaten by the expectations and rules beneath which all young boys must constantly labor. I, too, was still smarting from the pangs of trying to grow up too soon in a world that seldom cares, rarely understands, and hardly ever pays attention.

The more I thought about it, the more I began to identify with those students who hadn't made it out alive. I realized that I'd had to destroy, crush, and bury important parts of myself along the way to adulthood. And as I mourned the lives that were taken much too soon, I began to mourn myself, the "boy" that I'd once been and have long since forgotten.

After the networks finished dissecting the Columbine massacre, giving viewers a round-the-clock view of the kind of terror and violence few of us will ever really know, an arsenal of personalities, psychologists, and politicians were called in to make sense out of the madness. Many of their egos, voices, and platforms still ring in my ears today. Blame it on the media, they said. Blame it on the parents. Guns, those are the real culprits. The arguments were as well thought out as they were carefully researched, and as a graduate student in psychology, I could understand the need to try to explain, identify, and analyze. But in the end, after all the opinions had been weighed and the votes had been tallied, the consensus was that we have to pay more attention to "our boys."

No matter how little time we have or how many defenses we have to break down, we must find a new way of communicating with the young men who will one day be the leaders, the educators, and fathers of a new generation. I feel as if I know all of the boys who contributed to this book personally. And all it took to get to know them was a friendly gesture, an invitation to speak. You see, our boys are willing to speak out. All we have to do is listen.

Our Inner Circle

In You We Trust

MANY OF YOU are going to be shocked by what I'm about to say, just because it is an extremely uncommon sentiment, but here it goes: I cannot think of one bad thing to say about my parents.

Now don't get me wrong, it's not as if there's never been any discord between us. Sure, we've had our share of disagreements, times when I would have gladly stomped out of the house or thrown a vase at the TV. But I never did do that. Why? Simply because I always knew that no matter what the subject of contention, my parents were always arguing from the viewpoint of what they thought was best for me. This made it very difficult ever to stay mad at them for too long.

The truth is that in their relationship with me, my parents have always behaved in the most unselfish manner. For as far back as I can remember, whenever I needed anything, whether it was a ride to soccer practice, help with my schoolwork, or advice on a relationship I was in, they were there for me. Forever putting my needs before their own, my parents acted as if they couldn't truly be happy unless I was.

However, having parents who fit the above profile does have

one main drawback. In a word, guilt. We're talking capital *G* guilt, colossal with a capital *C* guilt. No two ways about it, since I had the ideal parents, I *had* to be the ideal son. That meant never getting into trouble at school, never hanging out with the wrong crowd, and always striving to achieve the best grades.

On the rare occasion that I did transgress the boundaries defining my self-imposed perfection, I suffered great anxiety. The only way to relieve myself of these feelings was to push myself harder and make my parents proud. In essence, the avoidance of guilt acted as the main motivation for my academic and social successes. Anytime I would find myself in circumstances that involved making an important decision, whether it was to take drugs, get into a car with someone who had been drinking, or simply procrastinate when I had to study for finals, I always thought of my parents. What would they want me to do? How would they feel if something harmful happened to me?

Answering these questions was never too difficult; the hard part was actually conforming my behavior to them. Although I've been known to stray from the path that bore my parents' seal of approval, most of the time my course of action has been in tune with their wishes. Frankly, I could not bear to think of the heartache my parents would experience if one of my decisions had had ill-fated consequences. The notion that constantly haunted me when presented with a risky proposition was "My parents have always done their best for me, and this is how I repay them."

My parents were not strict disciplinarians; my choices never reflected a fear of punishment. It has always been the guilt. I tried to think of their well-being over my normal coming-of-age impulses. When contemplating my adolescent years I realized the great influence my parents had on me as well as my attempts to model their own behavior. Our relationship had become wholly symbiotic—it was as if I couldn't truly be happy unless they were.

The bottom line is that no matter how flawless our relationships with our parents are, the absence of conflict can be a problem in its own right. Take the essay "Dysfunctional Mediocrity" from Chey Pesko, for example. The writer sets up the story as he would a movie. His poker buddies are the ones with the "real" problems. Chey is just an observer, watching the action from a safe distance. In his poker game, good families are as rare as good hands, and Chey feels as guilty as if he'd cheated misfortune at his friends' expense.

The next story, "The Game," by Joel Ashcraft, also depicts a happy childhood. Joel talks about how his relationship with his father has enriched his upbringing, instead of focusing on the ways in which this bond might have alienated him from some of his less fortunate peers. In fact, while there is indeed a downside to growing up without any major family turmoil, the stability and joy that a solid family provides are priceless treasures that Joel, much like myself, wouldn't trade for the world.

In writing the pieces that appear in this book, many of the boys were very open about the problems afflicting their homes. Of course, such uncensored self-expression is the exception rather than the rule when it comes to our behavior in the real world. Whether our home life is "satisfying" or "dysfunctional," we all see our own families as somehow abnormal, and live in fear lest someone discover our dreadful secret. After requesting that his last name be kept anonymous, Jason describes a typical scene at his besieged household in "America the Beautiful." While the chaotic scene should strike a chord with anyone whose house is ruled by pain, anger, and resentment, it's Jason's ability to see past his own selfish needs and empathize with the rest of his family that makes this story so excruciatingly heart-wrenching.

The poem "Junkyard," by Mike Grohsman, picks up where the preceding selection leaves off. As his childhood lies dying a painful death, the speaker explores issues of abandoment and loss. He is unable to save himself, and has long since given up any hope of his family coming to his rescue. Unwilling to blame his father, Mike gives him credit for trying his best. But in the end, he believes that both of his parents turn a deaf ear to his distressing cries for help.

The next story probes beneath the surface of a family home to find a morass of secrets and lies. Dave Langley's essay "My Dad's Trippy Psychedelic Room" probes into the dark corners of the family basement, where he discovers his father, a war veteran, reenacting a scene from his days in the service. Scared and confused at what he finds, Dave runs away from the sight of his father's pain. While Dave is unable to understand his father's experiences during the war, what is particularly sad is how father and son deal with the aftermath. Unable to discuss the occurrence openly, the grown man and the little kid both choose to pretend as if nothing had happened and go about playing the part of a "normal" family.

Of course, all families have their share of problems, but the next stories dealing with divorce and single-family households reveal issues specific to children of broken homes. Jeffrey Dussich's "13 to 40" is one of the most insightful and painful accounts of divorce that I have ever heard. As it chronicles how he was forced to grow up too fast and adopt the role of "referee," Jeffrey's tale of struggle reveals the ravaging effects that an acrimonious divorce can have on kids of any age.

The next memoir, "The Hard Side of Life," also provides a rare look into the life of a troubled family. Shuffled between his biological mother and various foster homes, the writer is the victim of senseless abuse and perpetual loneliness. His quest to find a real home has yet to end, but we pray that he will one day find the love and support he deserves.

The last essay comes from Robert. It is through his eyes and painful experience that we can finally come to understand that he is not unique. Millions of young boys like him are left to fend for themselves. And without the proper parental figures to guide their way, they end up dealing drugs, abusing illegal substances, committing crimes, and landing up in jail. Fortunately, Robert's story has a happy ending—the perfect ending for this chapter.

> **Chey Pesko,** 18, Wantage, New Jersey

DYSFUNCTIONAL MEDIOCRITY

What a shot this would be—I mean, if anyone I knew ever saw me where I am now, I would be categorized as some prime-time junky from some life beyond reproach. I mean, this is a scene right out of some cheap mobster movie. First, the slow circular pan of the apartment, which reveals scattered garments and an occasional beer stain on the carpet, not to mention accumulated dust in hard-to-reach places. A table made of finished oak comes into focus.

Ambient movement interrupts the silence of the large room, as the pan continues from each tightly situated chair to the next, revealing one new face after another until completing the journey, coming into focus on the five individuals chattering like angry penguins. The dim, depressing lights leave grim shadows on each figure's face, leaving specific features like eye color and complexion just out of visual reach. The familiar stench of multi-brand tobaccos, ranging from the trendy GPC brand cigarettes to the wooden-tipped Jewel brand cigars, completes the mood for the attendees of this gathering. Zooming in on the blackened ashtray, there is still physical evidence of a previous encounter of sloth and ill demeanor with the carcasses of old, half-smoked butts, each with its own unique past.

The jagged cut to the next shot imparts meaning to the whole tomfoolery of the scene. A single pack of Juggler playing cards rests on the table, sitting vertically, as if attentive and listening to every word pouring from the flamboyant table. A pair of eyes fixate on the anxious deck of cards and, as if in slow motion, a clammy hand crawls its way over to retrieve them. The stage was set, the effects were right on, and, as if a quiet voice whispered into my subconscious, "ACTION," the table exploded into a lawsuit waiting to happen.

"Five card poker, jokers wild," announced the dealer as he looked blankly in front of him.

"I think we all already knew that, Jim," a voice answered back from across the table, in megaphone format. "We've only been playing the same game, every Saturday, every month, for the past year!"

Jim looked across the smoky table and eyed the dim face staring back. It was Matt, a tall, lanky teen who lived in this apartment with his father.

"It's expected of the dealer to announce the game before any cards are dealt," Jim barked back in defense. "It's the cardinal rule of the Dealer Guild."

I couldn't help but chuckle at that remark.

Jim quickly glanced at me, before turning his eyes back on Matt. The remaining two individuals at the table, who to this point had stayed out of the ordeal, both let out strange half-laughs.

"What's so funny?" Jim said immediately. He looked like he was getting agitated. His eyes darted about the table, looking each of us in the eyes. He began to breathe heavier, like an old vacuum cleaner. His face was turning a tinted pink.

I immediately ceased my amused behavior and slowly leaned back into a relaxed position in my chair. Jim was about to blow.

"Well, I'm a member of the Bullshit Guild, and I say you're full of shit," Matt barked back like a junkyard dog. He started smiling and leaned back on the rear legs of his chair.

Jim jumped to his feet. What happened next occurred in a matter of seconds, but the events seemed to unfold in slow motion, with each movement enhanced and magnified to the smallest detail.

I watched as Matt's facial expression morphed from one of glee to puzzlement. His eyes squinted and his jaw seemed to drop to a level. Jim clasped the nearest inanimate object, the Juggler card deck. I was amazed at his form when he wound up his arm like a real-time major league baseball pitcher. His long arm extended and the force of fifty-four tightly packed cards shot from his sleeve like a cannon. His wrist added a sick twist to the aerodynamics of the rectangular deck, sending it spinning wildly like a Chinese star. The deck homed in on Matt's noggin, striking him in the center portion of his fore-head. Still practicing his chair-balancing technique, Matt fell victim to gravity as the force of the deck sent him reeling back, arms and legs flailing wildly. I stood up just in time to see Matt's impact with the red carpeted floor. The room went silent and the scene then seemed to be put on pause.

Jim quickly attempted to compensate for the outburst by walking around the table to where Matt was lying totally sprawled out and looking at the ceiling. I also inched my way over to the crime scene.

"Why . . . did you do that?" Matt asked the air in front of him. There was a red blemish on his head, which appeared to be the extent of the physical damage. I reached for the deck of cards, which had landed a few feet away after it ricocheted off Matt's cranium.

Jim grasped Matt's arm, raising him to his feet. "I'm . . . I'm sorry. I just . . ."

He was quickly but politely interrupted. "I know you're sorry, but that's not what I asked. I'm looking for a 'why.' " There was a pause. "We've always joked like this."

Matt picked up his chair and sat down. Jim stood in front of him, like a criminal being questioned in court. Without an-swering, he turned and slunk his way back to his chair at the table. I mimicked his actions, and sat down myself. Lifting the cover of the deck, I removed the set of cards from within. A joker was on top.

Finally, Jim sighed and began to speak. "Man, when everyone was laughing at me I felt like a damn idiot. And there you were, the ringleader, orchestrating the whole thing."

I watched them closely. They were looking at each other, and the other two were busy talking about some freshmen girls, and how it "just wasn't right" for seniors to hook up with them. We were all seniors at the table, but they were speaking for themselves. I dropped the joker into my lap and began shuffling the cards on the table.

"I get enough of it at home. You know the way my dad is. Whenever anyone is over, he makes a damn fool of me."

" 'You're lying out yer' ass,' " Matt mimicked, trying to portray the sound of Jim's father. "I got ya. I guess it's me who should be saying sorry. Let's play some cards."

"What game?" I asked, smiling sinisterly.

Matt shook his head at me, and smiled a little. Jim actually smiled, too. Jack and Drew, who had been engulfed in their own conversation, both looked up. Jack pulled out a pack of cigarettes, took one, and threw the crinkled soft pack at Matt. Helping himself, he then threw the pack to me. I pulled a thin body from the near empty pack and continued the rotation. I pulled a Zippo from my pocket, lit the cigarette, and put it on the table.

"Bets," I announced. I fondled the lighter and studied it closely. It was black and well worn in. It had been through a lot; it had been with me when I moved, it had been lost between the tightest of car seats, and was even in the ocean at one point, when I was in the Bahamas on vacation with my family. Written on it in big red letters outlined in yellow was "POW," like in the old *Batman* series when the villains were socked in the face. To me, this antique was a symbol of power.

"I don't even feel like going home tonight. I think my dad's home. Can I bunk here tonight?" Jim asked, as he threw a gold-plated money clip on the table. It had the initials "J. R." on it. Joe Richards, I thought to myself, " 'Jim's dad!' "

"Yeah, why not. You know the way it is here," Matt responded in a restrained voice. The smoke from his cigarette was getting in his eyes and they began to tear. I stood the lighter up straight in the center of the table. As my hand retreated back to the deck everyone began digging in coat pockets like pack rats. Drew pulled out a small vodka bottle and rolled it to the center of the table.

I cackled and asked, "Where'd you get that, a hotel mini bar?"

"I stole it from my parents' liquor cabinet," he answered hoarsely.

"I wish to veto your bet, under the cheapness clause," I retorted.

"What's that supposed to mean?" he questioned.

"He means your bet blows. It's worthless," Jack cut in. "I think we're all in agreement here."

Looking around, Drew saw that everyone was nodding. He grabbed his bet and put five silver dollars, which seemed to be pretty old, in its place. He looked at Jack, who seemed amused. "Well, what do you have?"

"I'll find something," Jack responded.

He pulled out a long silver necklace and held it dangling in the light. We were mesmerized. The light danced all over its surface, blinding me when it caught the right angle. I took the last drag of my cigarette and buried it with the rest of the butts in the ashtray.

"What is this?" I yelled with my arms spread wide. "We come here to play some poker every Saturday, and every Saturday you guys use it as a reason to raid jewelry boxes, wallets, and liquor cabinets? What do you have, Matt, your mom's wedding ring?"

Realizing what I was saying, I calmed myself down and smiled like it was a joke. Buying it, they looked at Matt, eagerly, awaiting his bet. He looked at me and got to his feet. He made his way over to his jacket hanging on a hook at the front door and began rummaging in the pockets.

"You could have been a little more prepared," Drew quickly added, as he blew a smoke ring into the smog-filled room. The halo of smoke quickly dissipated into the existing cloud that seemed to hover above his head like a bad conscience.

Matt found what he was looking for and yelled over his shoulder, "Hold on!" He made his way back to the table holding a small black bag with a drawstring, sat down, and started to untie it.

The bag seemed full enough to supply Matt for fifty hands of poker. I was getting frustrated with the slow pace of things. I looked at the alarm clock sitting a few feet from me. It was blinking 12:00 midnight. What? These people have no sense of time here?

"C'mon, the suspense is killing me," I laughed. By then his hand was in the bag and he was feeling around. I looked around the table and saw that my friends were experiencing the same anguish as I was. Matt's hand stopped moving and it started to make its way to the brim of the bag.

"I saw this in the front seat of a parked car at the Getty station," he said. "I just had to have it."

I watched Jack's eyes widen, for he was closest to the mysterious bag. In Matt's hand was a small gun, black with a chrome-like grip. I eyed the petite weapon of destruction, and realized that this gadget wouldn't suit a midget, if anyone at all. He put it in the pot, where the rest of the bets were.

"That's no gun!" I exclaimed, grabbing the pistol to further examine it. I caressed the gun's cold grip and took notice of its light weight. I aimed it across the table at a picture on the wall. With the crosshair on a photo of Matt's family at Disney World I pulled the trigger and, as if by magic, a blue and red flame emitted from the barrel. A smile came over my face.

"Now this is a power lighter," I thought out loud, but quiet enough not to attract attention.

I laid it back on the table with the rest of the bets. Although stolen merchandise, the gun lighter captured my undivided attention. Groping the joker in my lap with my left hand I realized that the gun would be mine before the night was over.

The cards flew from my fingertips to each awaiting set of hands. Even I was amazed at my precision. First one, then two, faster and faster until five cards had been distributed to each of us.

"You thought the gun was real?" Matt laughed. He took a stealthy peek at his dealt hand.

"At first," I began, "but only at first." I, too, took a look at my cards. What a hand: a two of diamonds, a queen of hearts, a jack of hearts, a seven of hearts, and a six of hearts. I threw my hand down in disgust.

In all our history of playing, nobody had ever had a decent hand. No royal flush, never five of a kind or full house, merely pairs and triples. We really don't even know the complete rules of poker. We just enjoy the betting.

"I'm out next weekend," Jim said, while signaling me for two cards. I grazed the surface of the deck, sending two cards flying in his direction.

"Watch it. Someone might see 'em," he blurted.

"What's going on next weekend?" Drew said, while raising three fingers. I carefully removed three cards from the deck and placed them in the middle of the table. He snatched them and put his "losers" in a separate pile.

"I've got to go see my mom in Connecticut. She just got engaged."

"It's no big deal," Jack said gruffly, "My dad is remarried and I haven't even met his new little wife."

"You mean your step-mom," Matt added.

"Not the way I see it," Jack said sloppily, launching saliva across in my direction. Those damn *S*'s always get him, and we have to suffer because of it. He signaled for three and I quickly exchanged them for his discarded cards. The last thing I wanted was for him to speak to me in close quarters and bathe me in his lethal ooze.

"Matt, what do you need?" I asked.

Matt looked up and shook his head.

"I'm good," he responded.

He looked down at his hand and a small discreet smile came over his face. What could he possibly have? I was not about to lose my lighter and that gun in one worthless hand of poker. I quickly discarded my two, six, and seven. I usually stick with royalty, hoping to double or triple up. I grabbed three new cards but didn't look at them.

"I raise," I said bravely, throwing a dollar on the table.

That's the way we usually work. Start out with the big guns and work our way down with smaller bets. I turned to Jim, who seemed a bit bewildered by his own hand.

"Call," he droned, also putting a dollar on the table.

He was obviously out. He was a bad bluffer and everyone knew it. We all smiled at him. I gave him the "cut throat" signal and he snapped.

"I'm dead," he said sheepishly, grabbing his dollar from the pile.

I leaned back in my chair comfortably, knowing that I had one less threat to worry about.

"Raise," Drew said, taking out the vodka bottle again, rolling it back onto the table.

I looked at Jack's face, but his mind was elsewhere.

"You know what's funny. My mom drove my dad and me nuts. And when he left, he didn't even offer to take me," Jack started. "By the way, I fold," he announced as he threw his hand down in front of him.

I stayed silent. I mean, what could I possibly have to say? I couldn't relate. I couldn't relate to any of them. My parents had been married from the dawn of time. I began to feel a little uncomfortable. I glanced at Matt, who was midway through a yawn.

"Parents are unpredictable," Matt said, as he tossed a fiver onto the pile. "I think they're all crazy. They get together, have kids, and then fight about what to do about them."

He paused and looked down at my hand, which was still clutching my three new cards, still facedown.

"I'm not ever getting married!" he added.

"I hear you," Jim said agreeably.

By this time I was feeling a little nauseated. I made it appear as if I was shifting out of an uncomfortable position, causing my mysterious left hand with the joker to join my right. But just as I was proudly smiling at my own discretion, I looked across the table to see Drew staring at me. Was I busted? I studied every detail on his suspicious face. His thick unibrow slowly turned into a V and a couple of rolls appeared above his nose.

"My dad cheated on my mom," he began, "Isn't that the lowest of lows?"

Was it my imagination or did he put some emphasis on "cheated"? How could he have seen me? I was so smooth! I looked over at Matt, who was smiling at his hand. His bluffs were hard to call.

"Cheaters never prosper. Right, Drew? Your dad was eventually busted, right?" Matt asked.

"Yup," he responded.

Sweat began to bead on my forehead. A drop of perspiration actually rolled off my brow and down to the end of my nose, where it gathered, increased in size, and started to stretch and bob up and down. What would happen if *I* was caught cheating? It would be the end of poker and trust! The disturbingly large drop broke free finally, falling in front of my face. It homed in on my hand of cards, striking the smiling joker in his little hat. I watched the droplet stream down its face.

"How's your family life?" a voice boomed.

I looked up out of my daze at Drew.

"Who, me?" I asked innocently.

His eyes answered my question and so much more. I felt the sting of resentment on my conscience. I didn't answer. I lowered my hand and dropped a ten of spades in my lap. He was not on to my joker scheme at all, but I began to wish that he was. After all this time, after all the looks and comments, it became apparent why. Every Saturday, every week, we would meet and it was the same thing: home-life horror stories. There I was, the only "normal" one. My parents had a successful marriage, and had successfully raised three children. Family feuding was scarce and there was no hitting or cheating. On weekdays, we would all actually sit down and talk at dinner, the old "how was school?" and "what's new?"

I put my hand of cards down on the table. As I laid them out in a special order, I felt my body go tingly, as if judging eyes were piercing my skin. The cards read, ace of hearts, joker, queen of hearts, jack of hearts, joker.

"Royal flush," I announced barely above a whisper.

As I watched the remaining players at the table hide their cards in embarrassment, I never felt more alone. I felt naked and out of place. I reached out and clasped the pile of weaseled goods with one hand and dragged it in front of me. As I transported the loot bit by bit into my pocket, I heard incoherent voices all around me, like the adults on those Charlie Brown specials. I paid no attention to them. I actually started to wish my family was a little dysfunctional; I wanted a gruesome father to hit me after he drank too much or maybe a cheating mother to resent; perhaps just the acknowledgment that I was a mistake that shouldn't have happened. Then I would have something to talk about with my friends, and then I would be able to relate and talk with them on the same level. Otherwise, I'm the outcast with the irregular family and I'm the one who doesn't fit. Silently contemplating these ideas, I

look at my friends, one by one, and I come to accept the fact
that dysfunctional is now orthodox.

> **Joel Ashcraft,** 17, Congers, New York

THE GAME

My father and I have been playing each other in basketball
for as long as I can remember. Growing up, when I was
smaller and had basically no skills, he taught me and guided
me through the game. Even though he usually beat me, except
for the times when he felt sorry for me and would let me win,
just so that I would feel better, it was all right, because I was
learning. The more and more we played the closer I became
with him. Through this game of basketball we grew to be more
than father and son, and rather more like friends.

I remember one special day as we were playing out in my
driveway, in the quiet suburbs of New York City, when I was
about fourteen years old. It was a sunny, spring day, with a
slight breeze that made it the perfect temperature to run
around. My father and I had been warming up for about fifteen
minutes, and were finally ready to play ball. It started as most
of our games did with a little trash talking that was all in good
fun. I would say something along the lines of, "Come on, old
man, you can't keep up with my young legs." And he would
come back with, "Yeah, well you wish you could have inherited
my great basketball abilities, not to mention my stunning
looks," this last remark getting chuckles from both of us. As
the game progressed, we started to talk about life in general.
The deeper we got into the game and the higher the score
climbed, the more serious the talk became. He told me of his
experiences as a teenager growing up, and of all the problems
that he'd gone through. And I, in turn, told him about what

was going through my mind and what I had to deal with. Nothing was left out on this day.

On that little driveway that we called a court, I told him everything. I revealed my secrets and had no regrets about it. He was now on the same page as me, and our relationship was the stronger for it. We had come to a mutual understanding, and talked for about an hour afterward. He changed my life that day, showing me that I could be honest with him and that I had nothing to fear if I put my trust in him. Within a matter of two hours, our relationship grew substantially more honest than the average father-son relationship.

In case you're wondering about the outcome of the game, I won. And at that age, this meant a lot. More important, the game marked one of the first times that I really connected with my dad. It wasn't the last. In the two years since that particular game, I've safely confided in him on countless occasions. Whatever conflicts may come my way in my life. I know he'll be there for me through every step of the way.

> **Jason,** 15, California

AMERICA THE BEAUTIFUL

It's October 29, Friday, and I'm at home because I didn't want to go to school today. Last night, my sister and my father got into a huge fight and my dad threw my sister out of the car. I hate being in the middle of things because there isn't a right or wrong, just some ugly gray shit. We just came back from watching *American Beauty* and me and my dad were having a discussion about our interpretations of it. My father kept insisting that I couldn't understand all of it because I hadn't lived enough to have the experience to perceive what they were talking about. And I realized he was right, and I told him that he was. I guess that ticked my sister off, because she's at that age where she believes that we as youth are always right and adults are always wrong. My sister has so much hatred inside of her. Because my mom used to hit her a lot when we were younger, because my father's never been there for her, and because it seems as though my mother pampers me more. She has so much hatred inside of her, all she wants is to rebel, to hurt others like she's been hurt. And she couldn't take it that I was admitting that my father was right. So she started yelling at him, telling him to shut up. My father tried to sweet-talk her into calming down, and telling her that we all had a right to free speech. My sister went off telling my dad how his opinions aren't valid, and how he's stupid and should shut up, and they just went off on each other. Then all of a sudden my dad pulled to the side of the road and kicked her out of the car on the big hill by my house. I dunno who was to blame. My dad has never raised a kid. He's never had the experience of raising a child, and my sister's never known what it's like to have a father. Both of them have their reasons, and there is no right or wrong. My dad and I went back home to the apartment, and I talked to my mom and we went back to look for her. I just assumed that she wouldn't go back home because she was so angry. I'm so stupid and arrogant. Everything I do is because I assume that people would do the same thing as I would. I'm such an arrogant asshole. So my mom kept on looking while all I could do was sit in the car and read my book because I'm a heartless asshole. After a while, my mom couldn't find her, so we went back to the apartment so I could do my homework and my mom could get gas and try to look for her. I'm such an asshole. I walked into the apartment and found my dad yelling at my sister. I walked into my room, sat down and started reading. I just couldn't take it. Then my mom came in the apartment and my sister rushed to her, talking about how my dad kept on hitting her over and over again. I couldn't take it. I couldn't take it. It turns out that my sister walked home and was about to say sorry to my dad and he hit her. Then she rushed into her room. My dad barged into her room and started to yell at her, and she told him to "get the fuck out." Then my dad just went at her and kept on hitting her. And all the while my sister was explaining to my mom, I just sat there reading. And then I started shaking, all over my body. I couldn't stop it. I put the book down and curled into a ball to try to stop it. Then I burst out crying, because I couldn't take it anymore. I just couldn't hold on to it anymore. It blew up inside of me. And everything rushed back to me, how crappy my life was, everything. The bulimia—yes, I was bulimic for a while—the thoughts of suicide, the depression deep down inside, the suffering, and the sadness of knowing that life is pointless. Then my sister came into my room to go online because she didn't care anymore. My dad just proved to her that her hatred was justified, and she didn't care, she didn't care anymore. All I could do was cry, I felt so naked. So I yelled at her to get out. And I cried for my sister, who doesn't understand my father's suffering and can only feel hatred. I cried for my dad, who lives the loneliest life by himself knowing that he'll never be a success in life, and then comes home to a daughter that can't sympathize with him. I cried for my mother, who has given up on all of her happiness for me, who is consumed by sadness, and my sister, who is consumed by hatred.

▶**Mike Grohsman,** 17, Lodi, New Jersey

JUNKYARD

All of my dreams and smiles
Are buried in piles of junk.
Nobody tries to clean it up.
They just watch it rot.

Every minute that passes by
Helps my memories spoil.
Dying with each fight, each scream,
My childhood fades away.

Mother tried to clean the yard,
In the days that passed.
Now she doesn't have the time,
To keep her family alive.

Father still tries to help out,
Despite my mother's torment.
He is dumb, but he is kind,
Breathing life into what is dead.

A family is a cornerstone,
To every sane individual.
Where there is no family,
There is no happiness.

I am just a battered doll,
Thrown around by ignorant kids.
When new and clean, I was their love,
And now I am a mess.

So here I lie in this junkyard,
Decaying and suffering,
There's nobody to pick me up,
And clean off all the dirt.

The dirt from screams, the scars from tears,
They'll always be right here.
Even when my family leaves,
They will still remain with me.

> **Dave Langley,** 17, Mt. Prospect, Illinois

MY DAD'S TRIPPY
PSYCHEDELIC ROOM

I first came into this world to join my family in Niles, Illinois, on a street called Ebinger Drive. We didn't stay there very long, but even the short time spent in that house provided me with scores of half-memories. Many of these partial memories relate to specific places in the home, which seemed, at the time, to be an exotic and mysterious place. However, there was one area of the house that brings back the most memories, the basement. It wasn't an especially extravagant room, it had no furnishings, and it was very uninviting, but it fascinated me nonetheless. Basically, it was a dank, empty dungeon, and I found myself intimidated by it.

The strangest part of the basement would have to have been the small, doorless room in the far, dark corner. In place of a door, a cacophony of beads hung menacingly over the frame, swaying gently in the flat, mellow breeze. The beads were enough to keep me away from the room, but sometimes I raised enough courage to push them aside and look inside. Behind the love beads sat a haven for every prog-rock loving, Vietnam veteran American man. My father just so happened to be one of those men. Back in those days, I didn't really know much about Vietnam, but now I have grown to understand it a bit better.

There is one day in particular that I understand now much more than I did back then. It was a cozy, rainy Saturday morning, which meant that my dad would be home all day. After lunch, I began running around the house searching for him, desperately in need of a good game of Mr. Tough Guy. This, of course, is the game where children violently attack their burly father, knowing that they have no chance of hurting him, or even knocking him over. However, on this particular Sat-

urday, I was going to see a side of Mr. Tough Guy that I had
never seen before.

After searching through every room on the upper levels of
the house, I decided to descend into the depths of Hell. The
darkness enveloped the basement in a dark sheath of black,
and a strange, radiating, colorful light echoed out of "the
room." I slowly shuffled my moccasin-clad feet across the cold
concrete floor, until my back pressed gently against the dusty
brick wall. Very carefully, I peered around the corner. Not sur-
prisingly, the multicolored strands of hippie beads obstructed
my view, so I painstakingly pushed them aside.

I could hardly believe my eyes when I looked inside the
psychedelic room. Suddenly, my ears flooded with the sounds
of the Moody Blues, and I saw my father wearing his army
fatigues, engaged in a violent, jerking dance. Three lava lamps
churned away in the corner of the room, as a few small black
lights cast an eerie glow on my father's frightening exhibition.
Needless to say, I was scared out of my impressionable little
mind. Enraptured by my terror, I fell forward and rolled
through the entrance of the room.

It took a second for my father to come out of his trance,
and when he did, he was none too pleased to see his young
son sitting on the green shag rug of his private place. The
anger oozed out of his bearded mouth like steam from a boil-
ing pot of water. "David! Get the hell out of here!!! Damn it!
Who let you in here!"

His frenzied words brought tears to my eyes, and I scram-
bled out of the room as he clenched his mighty fist and lifted
it into the stale air. I quickly escaped my father's wrath by high-
tailing it to my own secret place, the crawlspace.

I think I hid in that cramped, musty cave for a few hours.
Eventually, I gained the strength to rejoin my family, and when
I did, I found my father sitting in his favorite easy chair, wearing regular clothes, reading the sports page. Grabbing a handful of cookies from the kitchen, I stealthily slid down onto the

carpet next to the easy chair and silently read the comics, a restrained laugh held tightly against the back of my teeth.

> **Jeffrey A. Dussich,** 18, Manhasset, New York

13 TO 40

Phone numbers, people's names, directions, or even specific dates are the kinds of things I rarely forget. October 23, 1994, will go down in my mind as undoubtedly the darkest day thus far in my life. I did not know it at the time, but that Sunday night was chapter 1, page 1, of a four-year-long and hurtful novel ironically entitled *The Best Times of My Life*. Obviously, the cliché used to describe the average teenager's high school experience never applied to me.

I can confidently say that no one enjoyed being a member of our family as much as I did. Although my parents' relationship seemed to be on edge from the beginning, I was more than satisfied with the facade that they created in order to tolerate each other for the most part. A fond memory is of playing football on the beach of our favorite hotel in Florida whenever we would go down there, which was as much as once each month. The teams were my younger brother and father, versus my older brother and me, and during these games my mom would sunbathe on a nearby lounge chair. During dinner in the evening, we would share thoughts and laughs about the day's activities, while showing off our recently tanned skin. This made me happy. Simple? Yes, but it was enough to make me feel secure in this crazy and often cruel world. I think it's easy to see why I enjoyed those football games so much. In a way, those memories are my main connection to the pre-breakdown era, and they have begun to represent true happiness in my life, or at least in my memory. I can smell the ocean and feel the sand, and now and then I get that feeling in my stomach that occurs after excessive laughter, which was a common aspect of those times. It is now, though, just a memory.

I remember going to school in my brother's car the Monday following that climactic day in my family's life, and luckily his music was deafening or else there would have been some awkward conversation back and forth. I hadn't slept much the night before because I couldn't help but hear the screams of anger and hatred, no matter how hard I pulled the pillow around my head. I heard the accusation but I wasn't ready to accept it, nor was I ready to validate the explanation or excuse. Was it my fault that I found the extra airplane boarding pass? Or was it his fault for leaving it to be so easily found in his pants pocket? I didn't know what to think, nor did I know what to do. All I could do was act as if this whole mess would blow over. Besides, I was still busy trying to make a good, first impression on the new friends whom I met in middle school. Bite my lip and suck it up; I just wanted things to be normal.

It didn't take long, however, for me to realize that this wasn't like any of the other arguments I've witnessed between my parents. My home, which was once a place of comfort and relaxation, turned into an all-out war zone, and the dirtier the attack strategies, the better. The tension made for an unbearable environment, and the mudslinging prevented any sort of frivolity. During the first two of the four years of this dark and ugly period, I refused to stay home from school with an illness, until I was finally hospitalized with bacterial pneumonia.

I couldn't stand the way my parents spoke to each other, and it was even worse when they didn't speak at all. The disgusting behavior soon rubbed off on me. I became bitter and nasty to my younger brother, who was clueless as to what had happened and what the fate of our family was. I don't think I was blaming him, but I used him as an outlet. This situation was affecting every part of my life, from schoolwork to relationships, and I couldn't talk to my usual social shrinks, my parents, because *they* were the problem. I began to dislike them more and more, and by the end of my seventh-grade year, I didn't even like being around them. I found their method of solving this problem to be childish, as well as extremely selfish.

When my older brother, Joey, left for college in the fall of 1995, the only person I could talk to left with him. My younger brother, James, was still too innocent to understand the details of why Mommy and Daddy were yelling so much. I was thirteen years old at the time, and the next thing I knew, I was the single parent of two bickering children who chronically fought and could not speak to each other like human beings. Literally overnight, I went from thirteen to forty, and suddenly, it seemed as if my emotions didn't really matter.

For the next three years, my position as a mediator presented me with many responsibilities, one of which was to be the official messenger between the two warring generals. I was given letters and verbal "telegrams" by each party to bring to the other, and was expected to bring back a response. I refer to them as parties now because they were no longer parents—they had become merely figures. Don't shoot the messenger? Well I was shot *plenty* of times in the course of this war. The next responsibility, of course, was to make sure any and all phone conversations and random physical confrontations, (e.g., birthday parties) ran smoothly with little hostility. Unfortunately, this was a job that even I could not successfully complete every time.

The next few years following my metamorphosis from adolescence to middle age are kind of a painful blur. I am not sure, though, if the blur is caused by a subconscious or intentional mental block, or just a result of the many tears that could only be shed late at night when I was relieved of my duties for the evening. I couldn't let my emotional guard down until just recently, when I was positive I wasn't in an extremely vulnerable position. I had involuntarily grown up too quickly. For so long, I'd been putting on a fun-loving and laid-back social face:

the kid that everybody liked. Inwardly, though, I was a mess—a wrecking ball of compressed anger.

October 15 of this year marks five years since I first lost my sense of true family. No one enjoyed being a member of my family as much as I did, because I took pride in the fact that we were together as a unit. Now that the divorce is finalized and the dust has settled, I reflect upon the experiences that have left me where I am today. During those especially tough times, I thought I would have surely crumbled, but it gives me a true sense of accomplishment knowing that I stood my ground in what has been characterized by the many overpaid lawyers as a "very ugly divorce." Five years later, I am left with a multitude of unanswered questions and plenty of unresoved issues with my parents and myself, but through all of the hurt and tears, I am proud to say I am still standing and going strong. I do realize, though, that the worst of the worst is behind me. So what if the *best years of my life* were spent as a referee? It's just a cliché anyway. I believe this was only a test of will, and that the best times are still to come.

> **Anonymous,** 17, Ukiah, California

THE HARD SIDE OF LIFE

I never had a father. My biological father left my mother before I was even born. The next man in her life was an abusive drunk. He beat my mother and me often in his drunken rampages. In the end, he tried to shoot me. Luckily, it was with buckshot and only a piece of the shot hit me. A bigger piece hit my best friend. I was only three years old.

After the incident with my mother's boyfriend, I went to a foster home. I stayed there for about a year and then my mother regained custody over me. We had some good times and she said she would never leave me again. The next thing I knew, she was hooked on heroin and was busted at a dealer's house. When the cops raided the house, they found me, an unconscious five-year-old.

I went to live with a foster family again. The parents of this household were Rhoda and Raymond. I ended up being adopted and living with them for eleven years. I came to love this family as my own. My brother Billy came and lived with us and things were great. Well, things were better than before. I still got beat up, but it was mild compared to the drunken beatings from before.

On December 28 things changed for the worse. My brother and I got into a confrontation with Raymond and his son, Ted. My brother Billy and I ended up leaving and staying with our sister Katherine. Ted threatened our lives and those of people that we cared for, so we left, not wanting to deal with a homicidal maniac.

We stayed with Katherine for about a year and then she got into trouble for having too many people in her house. So I left and stayed with my friend. It was only supposed to be for two weeks, but it's been a year now and I'm still here. My friend ran away but I stayed with his parents. I feel very out of place, but I stay and I wonder what will happen next.

▶ **Robert,** 18, Redwood Valley, California

I was born August 1981, in Red Bluff, California. My parents moved to Sacramento when I was about one. I am the oldest in my family out of ten brothers and sisters. My family and I went through hard times, living mostly in apartments and some nights having very little to eat.

As a younger kid in elementary school, I shared clothes with my little brother. Even at that age I hung around with "the wrong crowd." My mom told me that, but somehow I felt I belonged in the wrong crowd. I have seen a lot and done a lot of immature things we would consider wrong in today's society. Selling drugs, stealing cars, fighting . . . those are just a few of the worst.

As I look back I see that I didn't really accomplish much. Having to look after my younger brothers and sisters gave me a sense of how my mom felt and what she had to go through to raise me. I never again blamed her for the sad times I went through. I tried to make life good for my family, and to protect them from the things that I experienced.

To provide money for my family, I started dealing drugs at the age of sixteen. My father was lazy and didn't want to work and I hated him for it. I couldn't see how he could sit on his ass while his family went without food or clothing.

Around this time, my brothers and sisters got taken away from my parents. The courts decided that my brother and I were too old for a placement home, so he moved to my aunt's house in Covelo and I stayed with my mother and tried to support her during the hard times.

I moved to Covelo in the beginning of 1998. It was then that I got in trouble with the law and was placed in a group home in Redwood Valley. Now I live in a unique environment that supports and looks out for my well-being. The mutual respect that exists at this place has changed my way of thinking. Learning to create deeper relationships has changed my world. Before, my world was a three-block radius in Sacramento, and now I realize that I am capable of anything.

2

Sharing a Room

LET ME START OFF by saying I love my sister. This is the first time I've ever expressed that sentiment to anyone, my sister included. Although we get along fine now, our relationship wasn't always this amicable. For as far back as I can remember we've always been on each other's last nerve. Growing up under the same roof was a nonstop battle for supremacy. Even during times of cease-fire, our rapport was always marked by an aura of tension. Our relationship problems went beyond the classic case of sibling rivalry. Since we could never resolve any argument, trivial feuds over who got control of the remote or who would take the car out could easily escalate into cold wars that spanned months. Our relationship lacked the resilience needed for healthy communication. Far too obstinate to make any attempts at reconciliation, we would usually wait until a third party, usually one or both of our parents, got involved before resuming contact.

Now that I'm a little older, I can look back and try to analyze why we behaved the way we did with some measure of objectivity. In so doing, I am faced with the fact that many, if not all, of our problems were a result of my attitude. Since I am three years older than my sister, I felt that I was entitled to dictate her life. This combined with the fact that my sister has always been a very independent person, did not make for an auspicious association. I was too involved in her life, doling out comments on every decision she made, ranging from what music she listened to, to what types of guys she dated. Suffice it to say she didn't appreciate my active participation in her affairs. I can't blame her for often electing the zero communication option, given all the aggravation that the alternative must have produced.

The fact that my sister and I get along much better now can be traced back to an event that took place in the summer of 1996. My sister had just spent a semester abroad in Spain and had two weeks off before her return. My parents thought it would be a good idea for me to visit her and then for us to come home together. Even though I hadn't spoken to my sister in months, I accepted the offer. Who would turn down a free trip to Spain? Little did I know that those two weeks would forever change my attitude and behavior toward my younger sister.

Because I was in a strange country, did not know my way around and spoke no more than three words in Spanish, I found myself in a very unusual situation from the moment I got off the plane; for the first time in my life, I would have to rely on my sister for help. I had to rely on her for everything, from ordering my food to getting around town. In high school, it was I who took her around and showed her the ropes. And now she was my one link to the outside world.

The truth is, I resented her a little for that. I wanted to be independent and explore the city on my own, but as we took in the sights and explored the area, I began loosening up and actually enjoying having my sister as my own personal tour guide. I began to see her for who she really was, and my appreciation for her intelligence and her company grew with each passing day.

Once we arrived back home, our relationship was never the

same. We fought less and less, and actually listened to one another's problems. Of course, we still have some problems to work out and by no means is our relationship perfect. Old habits die hard, and no matter how much I try, I often catch myself reverting back to the old patterns. I can't help myself. I love my sister, and feel protective of her. I don't know if that makes me a bad person or not. All I know is that she'll always be my little sister, and I her big brother.

Boys' siblings, like their friends, have a profound influence on them. Whether they're nice or mean, male or female, siblings help us learn about what we're capable of as well as our limitations. The best-case scenario is when siblings get along and spare their poor parents the pain of having to hear them fight. Unfortunately, even the most loving siblings will tend to fight now and then.

Although I never had a brother, I could definitely identify with Jeremy Turnage's story about fighting over the remote control with his beloved little brother. Few families can honestly say that they've never been privy to this familiar slice of family life. When we're young, a thousand years of civilization is lost on us, but "might makes right" is a certainty we've learned in the school yard. It's no wonder that most parents have to either wait years or escape to a tropical island resort in order to enter a room without being confronted by a floor wrestling match.

Physical fights and arguments characterize almost every sibling relationship, but in "A Poisoned Family," by Andrew Huang, the threat of violence is much more grim and disturbing. Tired of his sister ruining the family's mood, the poem's narrator systematically plans a scheme to poison the troublemaker. He begins the poem with an angry tone, but as he plots the terrible crime, he begins to realize that he truly loves his sister. If anything, the idea helps him come to terms with just how much she means to him.

Sisters seem to be on everyone's mind. The writer of

"Change" adds another perspective detailing his woe at the prospect of his older sister's imminent departure to college. He recalls the times they spent together with fondness, and explains how much her kindness meant to him. His story shows us that even when siblings mature and leave home, they will always have a special bond that will unite them to the very end.

Last but certainly not least is Brian Hedge's touching essay about his relationship with his twin brother. He begins by explaining just how different they are. They have very little in common, including their musical tastes. But it is through pondering what makes him different from his twin brother that Brian discovers the strength of their family ties. Even though he can't stand the sound of his twin's stereo blasting through the walls of his room, he learns to appreciate it if only because it means that his twin brother is safe and sound in the next room.

▶ **Jeremy Turnage** 16, Beaufort, North Carolina

ADAM

What is it like to have a brother . . . Well, there he sits with his blond hair and what most people say are blue eyes, but looking closer you can see there's green in those eyes. He is picking up the TV control. There goes the finger! One push for power, and it's on channel 62. No channel surfing for him! No sir, it's the cartoon network all the way. Now to his chair, with that grin that shows some baby teeth and some bigger ones than that and also a few missing ones. Now here comes the blanket, and he is all set.

The look of contentment and happiness is shining through. Oh, yes! He's happy, and he's also got the TV control hidden in his chair so no one else in this family can get to it. But I'm bigger, so over I go. I got it.

I'm changing the channel. One scream! Two screams! "Stop it, Jeremy. I was here first." Those beautiful eyes and lovely grin are now full of hate and discontentment. Here comes the first punch, the fight, and Mom enters the room.

> **Andrew Huang,** 16 (13 at time of writing), Lebanon, New Jersey

A POISONED FAMILY

Can you see us?
Father, Mother, and Son
Do you see the joy between us?

You can't
There is none
We are all lifeless souls
Lifeless because of one being

That one being is but a single little girl
My sister
The daughter to my father and mother
But she is no real sister

For of her heart is cold rusted steel
And in her eyes is a burning, raging, flame
A flame that rises up from the deepest darkest pits
Only to make us hate her more

She has drained all the happiness through us
Out of our bodies, into hers
Taking our energy and giving back none in return

I am tired of my sister
She gives me great pain
That pain will soon stop
For I have a dark side too

A scheme has risen in my mind
A scheme to end it all
To end her life
To end our misery

I sit innocently by her
Having a sip of what will soon be her death
With a sudden abruptness, she stands up and leaves

My chance has come
The adrenaline rushes through me
As I silently slip drops of poison into her drink
With that she will soon be dead

She sits back quietly into her chair
Not knowing of the doom that will be hers
I stare down at her, as she takes the drink slowly
Ever so slowly
The cup rises to her lips
And the deadly poison runs into her mouth

A sudden snap of reality
This isn't right
She is my family
The only sister I'll ever have
I cannot let her swallow her doom
If I do
My life will have ended too
With the taste of poison in her mouth

She has to spit it out
So she has not died
And there is no more, a poisoned family

> **Anonymous,** 17, Ocean, New Jersey

CHANGE

My sister is the closest thing to me in my life, and when she left for college my life changed.

When I was a freshman and she was a senior, she gave me rides to school even though that prevented her from taking some of her friends. When I would have trouble with homework she would take time out from doing her work to help me. It's things like that that I miss the most about her. When she left for school last year things changed a lot for me. I didn't see much of her throughout the year because she would only come home on the major holidays. I would call her, but it wasn't the same as having her in the next room.

Going from having an older sister in my house for sixteen years to only seeing her five or six times a year is hard. When she was home, if I was excited about something or something funny happened during the day, I could always go into her room and tell her what was on my mind. Now I have to call her long distance or write her an e-mail. It's not the same. Even when she was home for the summer I never really saw her because she was always off working.

In some ways, though, my sister leaving has changed my personality for the better. Without her in the house I don't act like an annoying little brother anymore because there is no sister to annoy. I have learned to be a little more responsible and do things without her helping me. I know that my sister and I will always be close, but it's a change not having her around. I miss her and how everything used to be.

I can remember when she left for the first time last year, the two of us sat next to each other for the duration of the uncomfortable seven-and-a-half-hour drive to Virginia. Sitting in the backseat and doing stupid things to pass the time like we did when we were little kids, I felt as if this was just another family vacation.

When we got there and we were done moving her in, it was time to say good-bye. It wasn't like I would never see her again, but it was still sad. She started crying and we left. This year is her second year in college and I'm kind of used to having her away, but I always think about her.

> **Brian Hedge,** 17, Jacksonville, Florida

Yesterday was the seventeenth anniversary of the day I was born. I shared my presents and gifts with the one person who joined me in entering this world. Someone I feel I know better than anyone else does. The person with whom I share the same eyes, body stature, intelligence, and parents. He is my adversary, my motivator, my confidant, my friend, and my twin brother.

My brother and I are not what you might think of, when you hear the word "twin." Or for that matter even the word "brother." We have many differences. The one major difference that stands out in my mind is music. Like all teenagers, my brother and I listen to music. Our music selections, however, occupy opposite spectrums of the music world. I prefer slow moving songs, songs that have meaning and evoke emotion. My brother prefers music through which the only feeling you experience is the splitting headache throbbing painfully right above your left eye. My brother, who is an interesting specimen, obviously loves his music. Any negative comments meet with stiff resistance and any song my brother might like, or apparently adore, receives three more notches of an unnecessary volume increase. Our opposing views in music have kindled many a conflict, and my brother is notorious for playing loud music on nights when a distraction is least needed.

Sometimes I do not hear the music playing. No obnoxious lyrics or over obsessive bass line, but silence. No more AP physics homework interrupted by a rendition of "Brass Monkey" by the Beastie Boys, a band whose attempts at forging stanzas out of jargon are what my brother calls music, but actual moments where I can think and address my own thoughts. But the sublime thoughts that pour through my mind at these given moments are not of exultation and reprieve, but of loneliness and detachment. In these awkward moments of solitude with my thoughts, I come to an epiphany. I would not care if my brother played "Brass Monkey" a million times (which I am sure he already has), as long as the music never ends. It is the music that reminds me that he is there (two doors down from my own room) and that he will always be there.

I pause from my homework and look at the clock; it is nearly three in the morning. The music is off now, for it is late, and we both have school tomorrow. Yet, I am truly lucky, my brother is merely asleep and his radio will be on tomorrow.

3

To Friendship

WE WERE KNOWN as the posse. We thought we were so cool and, more important, we knew that everyone else thought the same. We'd worked very hard to arrive at this favorable consensus. We threw all the best parties. We dated none but the most sought-after girls. We hung out only with those whom we deemed worthy of our attention. Interaction with classmates outside of our social circle was to be avoided at all costs. We adhered to every stereotype of the elitist high school clique, and I'm sorry to say that, yes, we *were* proud of our behavior. In high school, as in life, it often seems that the higher the walls between your group and others, the more self-important you and yours feel. I bought into this insanity all the way until the second semester of my senior year, when I found out what my "friends" were capable of.

Out of all the guys I was friends with in high school, I'd known Adam the longest. Freshman year, he was one of the most popular kids at school. His older brother was a social giant and nepotism cast a strong spell over the student body, raising Adam several notches above the average cool freshman in the general esteem. If the legacy factor wasn't enough,

Adam had been blessed with yet another distinguishing characteristic. He was a year older than everyone in our grade—that's right, a freshman with a driver's license. While our fifteen-year-old contemporaries were cruising with Mom in the family truckster, or worse yet, suffering the indignity of regulation yellow, school district transit, Adam's friends were always sitting pretty. Adam had celebrity status at my high school; people would feel honored just to walk down a hall with him during school hours. So when he introduced me to his friends in the cool crowd, I thought that my standing atop the uppermost rung of the social ladder was pretty much carved in stone. Unbeknownst to me, that stone was as brittle and insubstantial as a scrap of shale.

The next two and a half years of high school saw me growing a lot closer with the new friends I had made as a freshman. There were four other guys I designated my "best friends" along with Adam. But as the years went on, there was a gradual shift in the group dynamics. When Adam's family life, appearance, and state of mind took a turn for the worse, his standing and influence within the circle ebbed, while my own flourished. But even as our calls to Adam's house were growing less frequent, we all still hung out together as if nothing had changed. By the time senior year rolled along it seemed like I was the only one out of the "infamous" posse to keep Adam abreast of any social events. Even though no one treated Adam any differently during school hours, I'm sure he could feel the tension.

The truth is that my friends were now trying to distance themselves from a person who they thought was becoming too boring and too complex for the high school social scene. I tried not to partake in my friends' occasional snubs toward Adam, attempting to convince myself that he was still one of my best friends. But the reality was that I'd begun to feel the same way they did. I like to think these emotions toward Adam took root in me because of how impressionable I was in high

school, not because I was truly starting to dislike him. The
reason I prefer to chalk it up to a weakness in an as-yet-
unformed character rather than to a malevolent nature stems
from one, isolated incident, an incident that taught me the
meaning of the word "cruelty."

At my school, like at most, the senior prom was considered
the event of a lifetime. Everything that surrounded this occasion was taken very seriously, especially the assignment of prom
limos. The limo you take to the prom is the last public statement of exactly who your friends were during high school.
That's why when my friends decided to exclude Adam from
our limo I knew there was going to be a problem. I had to
make a choice, either to go with them or with Adam. I resolved
not to go with Adam and take the limo my other friends had
rented. This was easy to rationalize, since I had been spending
more time with them and felt closer to them than to Adam.
Even though I would be hurting Adam's feelings, I told myself
he'd get over it and tried not to think about it.

Unfortunately, the story didn't end there. My popular
friends wanted to go one step further. They wanted to break
all ties with Adam. They felt he was bringing them down and
did not want to be associated with him any longer. Afraid of
risking my own reputation, I remained silent when my friends
bad-mouthed Adam behind his back. When my friends confronted Adam and told him that we didn't want to be friends
with him anymore, I again remained silent. I remained silent
while they pointed out all his inadequacies, while they told him
he wasn't fun anymore, while they said he should stop coming
up to us in school. And when he eventually cried, I still remained silent. That night was the most horrible night of my
life.

Saying nothing was just about the worst thing I could have
done. I wanted to defend Adam. I wanted to tell my friends
that they had no right to hurt another human being like
that, much less a former friend. But I couldn't. I didn't have

the strength. After the confrontation, I could barely stand to look at myself in the mirror. I knew what I'd done, and telling myself that it wasn't my fault was of no help to my guilty conscience.

During the prom, everyone was drinking, dancing, and partying. But all I could think about was that Adam wasn't with us. This was supposed to be the best night of my life, but I didn't enjoy it. I ran into Adam at the prom. He looked at me, and we both knew what was on each other's mind. But this time it was I who would cry. Not wanting anyone to see how upset I was, I escaped to the bathroom. The tears made my face red and blotchy, but my friends never knew the real reason I looked so bad that night. They laughed at me, saying that I had drunk too much. And just as I was about to laugh along with them, I realized that I didn't have to. High school was over, and so were most of my so-called "friendships."

It was Felix Flores's letter that started me thinking about Adam and the posse again. I'd thought that I buried those ghosts a long time ago, but reading Felix's "To an Old Friend" brought all those painful memories rushing back to life. All this time, I honestly believed that my actions had hurt me more than they had my friend. Now, I'm not so sure. Felix's despair over the loss of a friend coupled with the thought that I had been responsible for my own friend's suffering is what shakes me to my very core.

The next story, "Waiting for a Miracle," picks up the thread of friendship gone awry, but instead of focusing on the first torments of loss, the writer goes in a different direction, covering every aspect of the grieving process, from anger to sadness to eventual acceptance. An important lesson is imparted in the telling, a lesson about the fleeting nature of friendship between two people.

Michael Marino's poem questions the foundations of friendship. He wonders if his loyalty will be returned in kind, and decides that the only thing he can count on is his faith in God.

In light of the foregoing submissions, Michael's distrust of his fellow man is far from unfounded. We've all had, or have ourselves been, friends in name only, fine-weather friends who cannot be relied upon in times of trouble. Sadly, it is during our adolescence, at a time when we are just as desperate to project the right image as we are to connect, that we learn the pitfalls and shortcomings of these superficial friendships.

"Seeing Eddy Seawell," by Joshua Goodbaum, relates the tale of a friendship done in by circumstances. Two boys, alike in every possible way, bond over their shared dreams and aspirations. When Joshua goes on to middle school, he must leave his younger friend behind to fend for himself. Although this is where the friendship ends, Joshua goes on believing that the bond remains intact until some years later, when he sees what's become of his once vital and optimistic friend. The fact that the two boys barely recognize each other underscores the ephemeral nature of true friendship, and corroborates the message of "Waiting for a Miracle."

Change is the thread that ties these stories of undone friendships together. Change of mind, heart, or circumstance can easily disturb the delicate balance that is a relationship. In keeping with this theme Matthew Thompson starts his story by admitting to his chronic fear of change. In fact, he is all but forced into a change of scenery when his friend bails out of a summer college program in which they'd both enrolled. Confronted with new people and new expectations, Matthew's true personality is given free rein. Through his new friends, he learns who he is and who he is capable of becoming. While many of us don't get this chance until we move away from home, Matthew's is the true college experience. He'll never forget the friends he made during that summer, and, to be sure, he will never look at his past friendships in quite the same way again.

In "Restless Afternoon," David Sherman underscores the importance of true friendship in a young boy's life. Writing about his voyage into the forest, David shows that friendship is not a destination, but instead a journey shared by two people.

Eric A. Deleel's take on friendship follows a similar vein. He traces the strong bonds formed in early childhood, reminiscing on everything from getting caught smoking cigars with a friend to growing apart in high school. Like many of the writers in this section, he laments the passing friendship of his youth. He knows that time has changed the relationship, but still hangs on to the thread that will forever bind him to his childhood friend.

"Best Buds and Blood Brothers," John Heath's story about his best friend, reveals just how important a solid friendship can be to a young boy's development. Filled with details about the times they spent together, the story doesn't end with two friends growing apart. Instead, the two boys grow together and find that true friendship defies the passage of time.

Reading Edward Kim's essay, "Two Kids on a Football Field," I couldn't help but reflect on some of my own friendships. In his story, he describes the pain he felt upon first realizing that he and his friend had grown apart. The sadness and sense of loss he describes is something all boys can relate to. I remember a time when I discovered just how different my friends had become. I almost felt as if they had in some way betrayed me. But like Edward, I knew that I needed to remember the good times we had spent together, instead of ruminating on the pain of losing someone close to me.

Finally, Chris Chambers's poignant recollection illuminates the fact that the need to relate to our companions is universal. Say what they will about the shallow and monosyllabic qualities of male interaction, but the very fact that self-disclosure is so difficult for us, who are taught to never show our feelings and to always keep a stiff upper lip, is what makes it so key to the progression of our relationships. Once a friend *does* confide, it is as if the friendship is bound by blood and honor, there is no going back.

> **Felix Flores** 15, Winter Haven, Florida

TO AN OLD FRIEND

To You:

I don't know what it is that possesses me to pick up the phone and check up on you. Maybe it's the person inside of me who says he's moving on, but keeps glancing backward. Maybe it's my fear of losing my comfort zone completely. Or maybe it's the simple fact that I still care for you whether you care or not.

I tell myself to just forget you. To completely forget you, because it isn't healthy. Yet, every time I experience something new, interesting, good, or bad I want to share it with you and have your input, because no one listens anymore. I don't know if it is some quality I've lost that makes people bored of me or if they were never truly interested in the first place, but no one listens to my thoughts or ideas anymore. It could be that they never really listened to begin with and that you were the one that listened and that's all I needed. For the first time since high school started for me I have to work at making friends. They used to come up to me (those who saw I was new) and ask me questions and start a conversation with me and I never had to do anything, but be myself.

I'm still myself so I guess I've lost my charisma or whatever it was that set me apart from everyone else. That's OK, though, because I have confidence that someone will come around and see me in a different light than everyone else. Kind of like the way you did. I don't know why you did, but it changed things a lot. Too much to describe.

I don't understand you anymore; I don't understand me anymore. The only thing I want to do is share with someone who will listen. Just one person. I want to tell you on the phone what the chip on my shoulder is, but I can't take the risk of vulnerability anymore. I can't open for a while. I guess that's why I dream of being next to someone who feels the same way you did.

Why it is necessary for me to tell you this I don't know. All I know is that I'm in need of a friend. I know you probably can't help me in that department and I'm not asking either. I'm just asking for someone to at least pretend they are listening to my stuttering voice when my tears flow so hard I can't get my words out. In my world someone is reading this letter and caring that there was a voice that spoke these words to himself. Maybe you care. Maybe you don't. It doesn't matter anymore. It seems I've lost all faith in people. The funny thing is that I haven't lost faith in you. I guess that is why every time I hear you on the other end of the phone, and I know by your expressionless tone that you want to hang up, I hurt so deeply. Yet, I always call. Even if there are no kind words shared or any gratitude in concerns, gifts, or anything at all, I stab the knife deeper in my wounds and I call.

I still love you, but don't be surprised if I don't call for a while. If there is any energy between us at all YOU'LL call. I can only hope one Saturday night as I'm preparing to go out the phone will ring and that smooth, caring voice I once adored will tell me it is all right before I have to ask.

> **Anonymous,** 17, Florida

WAITING FOR A MIRACLE

P alm fronds were rustling lazily during that warm summer night on the San Pedro beach. The fans were whirring close by, and I could feel the humid air play upon my sheets. I was lying on a cot in a beach house located about a quarter of a mile from the beach, but I could still taste the salty sea air. Twenty rambunctious teenagers had spent all their energy during the last few fun-filled days, and all were now asleep, save one. The pain had become too much for me, and now, after months of intense agony, I was allowing my bottled-up emotions to slowly drain out. The rest of the group was sound asleep and there I was, sobbing softly into my pillow.

For you to better understand my situation, I must take you back a few years to the beginning of sixth grade. I had just moved from the small college town of Bloomington, Indiana, to a city named Abidjan, located on the coast of West Africa, in a country called the Côte d'Ivoire. When I first moved I was home schooled, which made it difficult for me to make friends. So when Sam reached out and befriended me, my life was changed. Our friendship took root in sixth grade and continued to blossom when I transferred to the international school that Sam attended. Together we spent hours riding our bikes around the neighborhood and buying candy from the shops along the road. Countless more hours were spent playing soccer, hunting lizards, and contemplating the cryptic female mind.

Disaster struck the summer before eighth grade, when Sam's family moved to Connecticut, where they planned to spend an entire year. I was completely devastated. Sam's move caused me to withdraw into myself. Knowing that he would return within a year, I spent my eighth-grade year simply waiting for his return. School lunches were spent in the library, and Friday evenings consisted of TV and books.

Finally, during the summer after eighth grade, the day of Sam's return came. I went out to the airport to welcome him, full of fear and hope. "I surely haven't changed," I thought. "But what about him?" That day, and for the rest of ninth grade, I found that Sam had changed. A lot. We did not "click" whatsoever. While I was literally dying inside for the chance to befriend him once again, he had absolutely no interest in rekindling our friendship. My waiting had been in vain.

Every summer my church youth group would spend a week at San Pedro beach. This was the first time that I had gone, and fun was mandatory. While everyone else was laughing and enjoying themselves, I found myself trapped inside of a shell that I had created, totally unable to relate to anyone except this figment of my imagination that I had once called Sam. Slowly and methodically I had cut myself off from others, and the moment I realized that the Sam I knew was never coming back I found myself completely alone.

The sobbing finally subsided, and I wiped my eyes one last time. I held my breath, listening to see if anyone had been awake to hear my weeping. I exhaled, thankful that no one had stirred. I slowly crawled out of the shell that I had been living in for the past two years and took a look around. My skin was sensitive, and I knew that it would take some time for me to become reaccustomed to life on the "outside." The experience had been incredibly painful, but it taught me a very important lesson. Friendship is a miracle that occurs between two people and can never be dictated. It took me two years to realize that nobody ever has friends, they simply are friends. From that moment on, miracles began to abound.

▶ **Michael Marino, Jr.,** 15, Valhalla, New York

YEAH SURE I'M YOUR FRIEND

Yeah sure I'm your friend. I'll be there when you fall just to
    pick you up.
To me, you are like a brother; nothing can come between us.
When you need money, don't hesitate to ask.
When you're in a fight, I have your back.
When you're homeless, I'll give half of my roof. When it's
    raining, I'll give you a ride home.

When you're hungry, I'll feed you.
When you die, I'll cry.
I'll be there when you need me

I also have a feeling that you don't feel the same way. What
    do I mean?
Well, to tell you the truth I can't trust you.
What I think is, you'll close the door when I'm homeless.
You'll ignore me when I need money.
You'll honk your horn driving by me while I'm walking home
    in the rain.
When I'm in trouble with other people, you'll take their side.
I also have the feeling that you'll kick me when I'm down
    and smile when I die.

Am I right? I certainly hope not.
Why do I think that?
Maybe because where I been there is no such thing as
    friends, only acquaintances.
Your own man could end up pulling the trigger that seals
    your fate.
The only person I can trust is my Lord.

> **Joshua Goodbaum,** 17, Madison, Connecticut

SEEING EDDY SEAWELL

A boy of nine, he chose a man's game as his own. Dressed
in his comfortable uniform of ill-fitting sweatpants, a rag-
gedy T-shirt, and a pair of run-down tennis shoes, and sport-
ing an unbrushed and cowlicked crew cut, he commanded the
chess board with the tenacity and skill of a man many years
his senior. Determined to succeed, he was thoughtful in his

approach to the game, patient in his movement of each piece, and deliberate in his strategy for every match. With maturity uncharacteristic of an elementary school student, he learned how to win, not only in chess, but in life, by playing the position his opponents gave him and capitalizing on every opportunity.

We were remarkably similar.

I first met Eddy Seawell when I was eleven. We attended the same elementary school and both belonged to a junior chess club that met every Saturday morning from 9 to 11 A.M. While most boys watched the animated X-Men and Batman and Robin battle their enemies on television, we studied the game we loved. Eddy's father, a tall man with thick gray hair unusual at his young age, organized the chess league and supervised the children who came, even though we rarely needed regulation. Chess players, even if they are children, are adept in self-control and discipline. Eddy certainly was. When we faced off over the chess board, he was never intimidated by me, despite my age, and we brought out the best in each other's games. We were both competitive, and our matches were fiercely contested, often ending in a draw or a narrow victory for one player.

When I looked at Eddy Seawell, I saw myself. We were both skinny and small for our ages. We were both called nerds by the other kids because we were concerned about our grades and participated in class; neither of us cared. We were not athletic, even though Eddy ran swiftly, and although we both played soccer and baseball through the recreation department, we prided ourselves on our intellects, on our abilities to use our minds in addition to our bodies. We enjoyed the challenge that chess presented, and we both approached it enthusiastically. We loved our mothers, admired our fathers, and respected our teachers. And we were determined to succeed in life, to become rich and famous and powerful.

Eddy and I often discussed our aspirations while we played practice chess matches.

"I'm going to be President of the United States," he promised me. "I'm going to run the whole world!"

"Only after my eight years in office," I said.

We liked to joke about the future, but our humor was far from sarcastic. We were both serious about reaching for our dreams, and we never doubted ourselves. We believed that the future held great success and that we had the ability to do anything we wanted. We were confident to the brink of arrogance, and we were stubbornly determined. I was sure that life would reward both of us for our determination and intensity.

My friendship with Eddy Seawell did not endure. I graduated to middle school and abandoned Eddy in elementary school. When the Saturday morning chess club evaporated, we lost touch. However, even though I no longer saw Eddy, I felt certain that we would meet again, perhaps at an Ivy League university or in the halls of Congress, but definitely in an illustrious atmosphere of tremendous international significance.

I saw Eddy Seawell the other day, as I was leaving and he was entering the bathroom at the high school we both attend. I doubt he recognized me because I barely recognized him. He was taller, of course, but he was different in other ways. His pale skin, which had always looked like snow during our chess-playing days, looked like chalk. Eric had long, unkempt hair that indicated an indifference toward more than just his appearance. He wore a baggy flannel shirt and loose-fitting grungy jeans that hung on his still-frail body as if he were a skeleton. He looked as though he used his clothes as a barrier, maybe to protect himself from a cruel world, but more likely to prevent anyone from scrutinizing him. I did not speak a word to him, and yet his meekness, his fragility, was apparent. He seemed to have lost his course.

Seeing Eddy Seawell disappointed me and wrenched a sense

of frustration deep within me. What happened to cause his dismal state? His mother could have died from cancer, or his parents could have divorced and initiated a contemptuous custody battle. More likely, though, he had succumbed to the pressure of life. In the conflict of every day, in the stormy weather that life can bring, he forgot who he was. He allowed himself to be defined by the thoughts and actions of others, and he failed to remember his boyish aspirations. He forgot his dreams. The realization of his failure, the revelation of his decline, saddened and hurt me.

As the door to the bathroom shut, I caught one last glimpse of Eddy Seawell, and an eerie thought crept into my mind. "Checkmate." I immediately regretted the idea, turned around the corner, and walked away.

> **Matthew Thompson,** 18, Ocean, New Jersey

FAR FROM HOME

Throughout my life, I have tried to avoid one thing . . . change. Somehow I was lured by my friend into going to a summer program at college. One way or another, he ended up not going. So there I was, left to face a new group of people on my own.

I still remember the day I arrived on the steps outside Porter Residence Hall. The laughing people and giggling peers that sat on the slab of concrete in front of the entrance frightened me. The air was cool, but the heat of summer was looming.

Using every last ounce of strength, I dragged my bags behind me. I made it to the elevator and dropped my bags off at my room. There I met my roommate, Kevin Duffey, known to his friends as "Duff." After talking with him for a while, I found that he was the person who could put every detail of life into short sentences, trivializing all the melodramatic tendencies of anxious youth. Duff had a few family issues, so the petty matters of women and social standing seemed not to worry him.

In order to meet some new people, we left the hall and went out to play capture the flag. Thinking I was someone else, a tall, preppy-looking kid came up to me. He had a calm, collected sort of approach toward people. He commonly forgot my name in the beginning, but he remembered it when he needed directions to his next class. His name was Mitch, and he introduced me to his friend John.

John kept mentioning how cool it would be to start a game of paintball in Beaver Stadium; he found joy in all the small aspects of life. He would go into the grocery store and read all the magazines for a half hour without buying one. And whenever anyone ordered pizza, he was the first one there to get a free slice. He seemed less serious, always looking for fun.

I sat next to Duff, Mitch, and John at dinner and met another new person. I was moving at an amazing rate, for this was the fourth new person in a day! Ben sat there in black clothing, with an attitude that could catch anyone's attention. He kept trying to match everyone's face with that of a famous person, and he decided that I resembled Wayne Gretzky. I insisted that I did not look like Gretzky in the smallest bit, but Ben's constant insisting stopped my opposition. He seemed as though he had control of almost every situation that life threw at him.

A couple of days later, I met Bobby. He was the kind of guy whose face would light up, and he'd start motioning with his hands when he got excited about something. He was the friendly guy that everyone could look back on in a desperate situation.

For weeks, we'd go about the trials and tribulations of the college social life. We were debonair and suave. We took control of the situation and made it ours. We controlled our destinies through the people we met.

It was then that I realized that I was no longer the shy and quiet stereotype I once believed myself to be. I inherited the best qualities of my friends. Duff gave me perspective. Mitch made me calmer and smoother in the presence of other people. John allowed my livelier side to show. Ben's flair made all my insecurities disappear, taking me to the pinnacle of self-confidence. And Bobby's influence allowed me to be more sociable.

Yet how was I capable of this? I have always believed that a person is who he is. People cannot change; they can only adjust. And then a second revelation . . . I had these qualities lying dormant inside of me. They had only just shown themselves.

▷**David Sherman,** 14, New City, New York

RESTLESS AFTERNOON

All friendships hit their plateaus sooner or later without any warning. How these altercations are dealt with basically determines whether the friendship dies or progresses. It was one of those afternoons where everything seems dull and boring. We couldn't for once find anything to do. I don't remember the exact details of how it started, but once in motion, it was like a boulder rolling down a mountain.

Looking back, I understand that young kids can get very restless, very quick. Very quick. Our impatience began to kick in and in a matter of minutes; we were wrestling in the center of his room. We had no real fight, no argument, and no bickering; we just fought for the lack of anything else to do. We were too young to actually hurt each other. I guess it was the release of a perpetual buildup of steam, accumulating for quite some time now. Our fight was not to the death. Once we had

exerted a large portion of our energy, we felt like we had re-
covered from a mesmerizing sickness. We did not hold this
against each other or our friendship would have been ruined.
To release the rest of this buildup, we decided to journey to
the outskirts of his property, a good distance from his house.

We walked through the tall grass and climbed through the
thickness of thornbush tangles. Josh and I descended the steep
gradient down the hill. All this time, we made it through using
teamwork, something I have learned to be essential in friendship and getting anything done. His property eventually ended,
but the land continued without a designated owner. We were
out there in the middle of the woods when we noticed three
deer no more than ten yards in front of us, staring us down in
terror. We were still, but I guess that deer can sense the presence of restless kids, so they pranced off like their life was
endangered. They had nothing to fear, though. We had come
out to the woods for no reason at all. There were no intentions
of harm or destruction. It never crossed our minds. Maybe we
were out there to experience what lay hidden deep in the
unexplored woods. Or maybe we were subconsciously on a mission to strengthen our friendship. For whatever reason we had
ventured into these parts, it was soon ended with a shout from
the house.

"David, your mom is here," she hollered, so that it echoed
in the silence of the forest, serving as a reality check.

The thick foliage prevented us from seeing far. All that
could be seen was the rising land up the mountain. We knew
which direction we had traveled (I had an incredible sense of
direction), so we began to double back, but going through
four-foot thornbushes again seemed impractical, now that we
were in a rush. Before, we had all the time in the world. Coming from nowhere and going nowhere. Time seemed as if it
had come to a stop while we made this important journey in
our lives. It didn't matter where we ended up; it was only important that we went somewhere together. Our circuitous path

led us nowhere, but in reality, it led our friendship somewhere. It grew with each step farther into this jungle of a backyard. Our friendship would never be the same now that we had taken this important step forward for the better of our companionship. We had learned so much about each other, and yet, there was so much more to learn. From this day forward, our linked lives would grow as one as we wandered into new parts.

This revelation brought us together, thinking as one. We found another path that cut across the hillside, getting us back to his house faster. We could have taken this route to the far reaches of his property, but that provided no challenge, no effort, and no energy. We didn't follow a bandwagon of people who took the easiest route to the end, never caring about anything. We were not like that. We took our own path and created a strong friendship based only on our own thoughts and interests. Something grew in both of us that day that encouraged our adventurous side, our courageous side, and our separateness from the rest.

After that day, we never had another squabble like the one we had that day. We learned something from that journey to the center of the woods. It touched us and united us in a new friendship that would not fail. From this point forward, I knew we would remain friends. It would last and go on forever just like our walk would. And though his property ended and there were limits set, nothing could restrict what had been created that day. There would be mountains and cliffs and rivers, all trying to hinder our progression. But we would overcome all obstacles and stay friends for life.

> **Eric A. Deleel,** 16, Massena, New York

UP IN SMOKE

M any people would agree that being a teenager is nearly all bad. Well, sure, as in many aspects of life, you have your ups and your downs, and this also holds true for being a teenager. Yet being a teen is not bad at all. There are many tough choices to be made, and there will always be the tough job of handling peer pressure, but it's worth it. I have found that through all the hard times, decisions, and tough choices to be made, you should always have at least one good shoulder to lean on. I was lucky enough to find my shoulder in second grade.

The two of us met in elementary. I remember the day perfectly . . . it was a warm fall day and the sun was shining brightly. . . . OK, so I made that last part up. Maybe I don't remember the exact day perfectly, but seriously, it must have been predetermined by someone that we were going to be best friends, because he was a year older than me. His parents had held him back for another year in grade two. We immediately bonded, and it was only a matter of days before I was asking my parents if I could spend the night at his house. As soon as I called him on the telephone, I found out that his house was right across the street, and his family had just moved in. This just furthered my friendship/fate theory that I have developed in my recent teen years.

Throughout our elementary years we were inseparable. We always loved to get up real early and walk through the woods in full camouflage, shooting at trees and small animals. This practice, although seemingly cruel to some, occupied a great deal of our time and also brought us a great amount of pride and satisfaction. For the most part, it was an innocent time, unless you count that one incident that involved two young boys and a couple of big juicy cigars. But there was hell to pay for that, and although my parents are clueless about the events that took place (needless to say that his parents were the ones who caught us), I still learned a valuable lesson. "Never trust anyone—even your best friend—when they say that their parents are truly gone for the night, especially when they say there is nothing to worry about." This is just a little life lesson I have picked up along the way.

Yet, when we hit junior high, it seemed as though we started to hang out less and less. Our classes in school were nearly opposite. We began to see each other only a few days a week and sometimes only on weekends. I'm proud to say, though, that through all the hard times we remained best friends, and anyway, things would always get a lot better in the summer, right?

It seems now as if those summers were a sacred time. What to us then was only childhood fun such as building tree forts and playing tackle football, are now some of our fondest childhood memories. There was never the problem of finding something to do. As it was, "something" would always land right in our laps. There isn't one thing he enjoyed that I didn't, and vice versa. This holds true to present day.

Now, I'd like to say that we are still best friends, and hopefully always will be. We stayed the best of friends through everything.

So as our bikes turn to cars, and our BB guns to shotguns and rifles, our hearts are still as young as ever. And although we kicked the cigar habit the first time we tried them, to this day we still get a laugh every time one of us turns to the other and says, "Hey buddy, you want a cigar? My parents are gonna be gone all night."

▷**John Heath,** 18, Madison, Connecticut

BEST BUDS AND BLOOD BROTHERS

I don't want to go to school, everybody's gonna hate me!"
I snapped this remark to my mother shortly after I woke
up to the first morning in our new home on Maryland's Eastern Shore. As an awkward seven-year-old boy, my outlook on
moving was far from positive. We had left our Stony Brook,
New York, home to settle in Maryland. I thought I would never
have friends the rest of my life and that everyone would laugh
at me for being from "Lonk Eye-Lint." The world was dismal,
but I did not realize that I would find my friend-for-life that
very same day.

My first day at school was worse than I had expected. I forgot my lunch, my book bag, and my courage. I sat alone in the
cafeteria while the other kids laughed and mocked me as the
outsider. My teacher forced me to introduce myself and give
my family background to the whole class. I wasn't picked to
play kickball during recess, although I was humiliated upon
being hit in the head by a runaway foul ball. A brute of a third
grader then tripped me and I fell flat on my face. I was laughed
at, I cried, and I wiped my tears as I held back the embarrassment bulging in my throat. After this day of mockery, I returned home with no friends.

To recover from my first day, I slouched depressed on the
couch and watched the Disney Channel. *Kids Incorporated* appeared dull and *The Mickey Mouse Club* seemed childish. The
television could not cheer me up, so I took a walk to explore
my new neighborhood. With dark clouds gathering overhead,
the weather seemed gloomy, but I continued to walk. I didn't
encounter any people during the first half of my trip, but that
soon changed. By the time I reached the middle of the neighborhood I spotted a large moving van in the driveway of a red
brick house. I ran to the house to discover the identity of my

new neighbors. I made my way up to the front door and rang the doorbell. A boy about my age answered the door.

"Hey."

"Hey," I responded.

"My name's Kent, we just moved here," he said.

"I'm John, we moved in yesterday."

"You wanna play?"

"Yeah," I answered.

Kent cheered me up and became my first friend in a new state. We connected like puzzle pieces and he made me forget about my horrible first day. Since that meeting, our connection has matured beyond a simple friendship: Kent and I formed an unbreakable bond. As seen through the eyes of others, our bond appeared to be a mere childhood friendship. Of course, we did play fort, hide-and-seek, and Nintendo, but friendship is more than childish games. Each day after school, I would run over to Kent's house so that we could embark on one of our many adventures. We walked for hours through the neighborhood woods and pretended we were kings of the forest with the world in the palm of our hands. We pretended we were Knights of Arthur's Round Table; we chopped wood together and crudely constructed our strongholds; we made swords from sweet-smelling cedar; we raked paths in lieu of a Yellow-Brick Road and used our BMX bicycles as stallions; we pretended we were hunters and killed the cold cuts and bread in our refrigerators for consumption; we climbed trees and were on the lookout for enemies; we gathered up pinecones for ammunition to use against any impending attackers; we gathered up kindling for a large bonfire, which measured a meager one foot in diameter; we placed marshmallows on sticks, pretending we were cooking pig; and we laughed and talked until the sun went down.

When we were too old for these fantasies, we moved on to more mature forms of entertainment. Kent and I played hockey together; we skateboarded together; we played basketball together; we threw the Frisbee together; and we created specialty foods together. The nutritious creations were the pride of our relationship. We raided our parents' refrigerators and plundered them for all varieties of meat, cheese, and other delicacies. We created omelets, sandwiches, and shakes, and entitled every creation the J&K Special. In the winter, we gathered pounds of snow and created snow cream—a creamy combination of powdery white snow, smooth milk, and rich chocolate syrup blended to perfection. We consumed each and every creation with complacency and enjoyed spending this time together.

During our middle-school years, Kent and I cemented our lasting friendship and we became blood brothers. We had heard about this term for a lifelong friendship one day as we watched an after-school special. In this particular show, two thirteen-year-old boys who have been friends since birth have formed a bond similar to mine and Kent's. One received straight A's on his report card, while the other struggled to get C's; one was always stern, while the other could never be serious. These two boys were quite an unlikely pair, but that is why they became blood brothers. They complemented each other so well, that they became more than buddies. Kent and I were awed by such a friendship—but then we realized that we had the same friendship as the boys on the after-school special. We watched the blood-brother ritual closely, in order to catch the fine details on how to finalize a long-lasting friendship.

The process of becoming blood brothers is quite an arduous task. The boys' ritual appeared easy to us: Boy A pricks the pad of his index finger with a needle. Boy B also pricks the pad of his own index finger with the same needle. Boy A and Boy B then place their bloodied index fingers against each other and hold this position for approximately five seconds. Boy A and Boy B then retrieve their index fingers and wipe away the blood using whatever T-shirt they are wearing (a white T-shirt works best for optimal stainage). When the epidermis of each index finger is clean of blood, Boy A and Boy B become blood brothers.

If only the process was that simple. Following the after-school special, Kent and I ran to his parents to tell them of our decision—"We want to be blood brothers." Kent's mom laughed at us and his dad pointed out the fact that we "will not do any such thing." His words mirrored something to the effect of "Haven't you kids ever heard of TB, HIV, or LMNOP?" We were befuddled by this usage of acronyms. We were just little kids and had no idea about diseases or viruses. Sensing our confusion, Kent's father sat us down and explained that we might get sick if our blood mixed together. We thought he was kidding, but we didn't want to take the risk.

Although we didn't want to risk getting a disease, we were still bent on becoming blood brothers. Following many minutes of brainstorming, Kent had an idea and rushed into the kitchen. Seconds later, he returned with a goofy smile, carrying a forty-two-ounce bottle of deep-red Heinz ketchup. Immediately, I understood what he had on his mind. We had heard, from all those Freddie and Jason movies, that the movie people had used ketchup to represent the blood that littered the floors of every room in every scene. If the big directors had used ketchup, why couldn't we? So, I grabbed some paper towels, and we ran off into the woods to perform the ceremony.

Deep into the woods, we chose a downed tree as the perfect place to become blood brothers. We sat upon the trunk as I placed the paper towels on the ground and Kent popped off the cap from the ketchup bottle. I became giddy with excitement as Kent held the ketchup bottle over my hand and proceeded to squeeze out the "blood." But the ketchup was stubborn and would not exit the bottle. Kent tried to conquer this roadblock by shaking the bottle, but the ketchup would still not budge. For some reason, he thought it would work best to hit the bottom of the bottle with his hand while the bottle's opening was pointed at my face. Needless to say, this time, the ketchup came out. It exited the bottle and shot toward my face as if possessed by a magnetic bond. Kent began cracking up and couldn't contain his laughter. To retaliate, I grabbed the bottle from his hand and gave him a ketchup makeover. Soon enough, we had dropped to the ground, wrestling, and rolling in a pool of ketchup. After a while, we had become exhausted, and gathered our breath as we lay on the ground. We couldn't help but laugh in realizing that we had become more than blood brothers. We had actually immersed ourselves, symbolically, in each other. Even though we didn't really perform the ceremony as originally planned, we succeeded in our own minds.

As food-making, ketchup-smearing Knights of the Round Table, Kent and I have endured as blood brothers. Even though Kent still lives in Maryland and I have moved to Connecticut, I still consider him my best friend. I believe that true friendship is when two people can be away from each other for years at a time and still be able to talk as if no time was lost. I have been away from Kent for four years, but each time I see him, we become closer and closer. When I go down to Maryland for a weekend, I always stay at his house and his family receives me with open arms. We spend the days together, seeing movies, traveling, or seeing other friends. When late night rolls around, we find ourselves in his attic bedroom, where we talk for hours on end. Absolute friendship is when hours seem like minutes and there is never enough time. Kent and I have a true, one of a kind friendship—we are blood brothers. Our relationship is evidence that there is no particular process to become blood brothers. We are best buds and blood brothers simply because we are.

>**Edward Kim,** 17, Manhasset, New York

TWO KIDS ON A FOOTBALL FIELD

Moonlight spills upon the vast field of titans where wars waged and battles fought. I peered past to the shadows of evergreens swaying with the elegant wind and I and he and we sat under moonlight upon this field swaying with the evergreens. We spoke the silence of many years and observed a powerful night in all its beauty, in all its independence, and in all its harmony. What field without the light of moonshine and where would evergreens sway without a wind so gracious? We sat upon the posts of glory and from this place we could see all for a hundred forever miles into the darkness. Cold winds are angry, the moon scared, the field lies and the evergreens die. But we sit here my friend and I in the dark where all is gone and we remain, remain to speak the language of silence.

There is nothing so precious as true friendship. Yet there are times when even something so precious must be sacrificed. This is the story of my friendship with Steven Sung from the beginning to the very end.

This is how it began. My first acquaintance with Steve was truly an act of God, or so it seemed at the time, being that we met in Sunday school. Of all the seats in the class, it was God, not the teacher who had placed us side by side. And from that moment forth, side by side we would remain forever. When you're only four years old, everything seems like it's going to last forever. Unfortunately, nothing ever does.

While the rest of the class was attempting to understand the ABC version of Genesis, Steve and I attempted to understand the ABC version of each other. And that's how it was for the next five years. Occasionally we would meet at each other's houses or a birthday party, but for the most part our friendship was limited to our encounters at church. Perhaps that is the origin of my devotion. That subconsciously I interconnected my relationship with Steve with that with God.

What happened next was proof that some things are just meant to be. In the summer before fifth grade, Steven Sung became my new neighbor. I vividly remember the moment Steve told me where his family had decided to move. We laughed and danced like giddy little girls. I also remember that was the moment of our first hug.

Within the first week of school, we felt it was necessary to differentiate ourselves from the rest of our peers. So emerged the Slick Brothers. Over the course of the next month we created a secret handshake and membership cards. The elaborate and exclusive nature of the Slick Brothers attracted a great deal of attention and envy. At one point, kids were begging to be dubbed a Slick Brother. Then life moved on, we continued onto middle school, and the Slick Brothers were soon forgotten. Nothing had changed between us since so many years ago. There was a reassuring stability in our lives that only brought us closer. Then everything changed.

In eighth grade, I moved to a neighboring town because my parents felt the influences of my environment were corroding my mind. We all experience an awakening at one point in our lives, for some it comes early, for others too late. At first, I resented my parents for separating me from everything I had loved. I retaliated by remaining a social outcast at my new school, eagerly awaiting the weekend when I could be united with my friends and Steve.

Gradually I began to reach out for companionship. Through the encouragement and support of various peers and teachers, I made a great deal of self-discoveries. It was time for my awakening. By the end of freshman year, I was writing poetry, in love with the cello, writing then singing and performing songs on my guitar, fascinated by abstract art, interested in the ongoing issues of the world, and infatuated by jazz. In the face of my attempts to make my ambitions his, Steve did not always respond with acceptance but sometimes with strong objections. At one time, our two minds had been one. Now, they were worlds apart.

I once said that some things were just meant to be. Perhaps this was one of those things. I wanted to experience the world for all that it had to offer. Steve was content with where he was. We began to see less of each other. The phone also ceased to ring with him on the other end. I have and always will love Steve no matter what may come, but now I must love him through my memories.

One December evening, I received a call from Steve inviting me to his house to celebrate his birthday. After I hung up the phone, I screamed in the agony of my own stupidity. I had priorly promised a close friend that I would attend her sweet sixteen. So I came to a compromise. I would stay for the first half of Steve's party, then attend the second half of the sweet sixteen.

Soft snow was falling from a starry sky. It was the first snow that winter and somehow instilled within me was a feeling of hope. Walking to Steve's house, I reminisced about everything that we had been through, how it had started, and how it would end. As always, I entered his house through the back door and went on down to the basement. Everyone else had already arrived. There is a great joy in being reunited with a circle of friends. I embraced each of my old companions and introduced myself to the new.

When I found Steve, we looked into each other's eyes, a moment so familiar that it was timeless. I then hugged him with all the love I ever had for my dear friend. As the party progressed, the environment became livelier and festive. I conversed with a friend but it was not Steve. He was with the new companions I did not know. At that moment, I conceived just how much things had changed between us. A piece of my soul died right then. Suddenly, I glanced in the direction of an energetic cheering and jeering. Steve and someone else were wrestling half-naked. I then realized it was time for my departure. I quietly made my exit so as not to disturb the tempo of the moment. Slowly climbing the stairs to the door, I wrapped on my wool overcoat and buttoned up all the way to my neck. The snow had accumulated a great deal, but the powder softness alleviated the burden of heavy steps. I stood to admire the beauty of the night. Each crystalline star shone with pride, the bare oak trees defined by the light upon snow so pure white. I pondered which street I might take to the bus stop and in every direction I saw an unblemished perfection. A moment before embarking, I turned up my wool collar and rubbed my bare hands raised against my lips while exhaling. The warm air froze, growing cold, no different from the rest. Initiating the first step, I started down the street.

"Whatever happened to always?"

The words cold as this night pierced my heart. A tear had penetrated my eye. And for all the pride I had so solemnly convinced myself of having, I could not cease this single tear. I turned myself toward the voice and there he stood, shivering, dressed solely in boxers and a T-shirt. His pale skin tinted red from the cold, or was it sadness? I walked toward him with heavy steps and stared into his dark brown eyes. My own eyes then fell upon the wool coat. I undid one of the buttons and reached into my inner pocket. Carefully I extracted a card with my hand and placed it into his while assuringly clasping it with my other hand. Again our eyes met. This would be the last time. Releasing my grasp, I walked away into the snow covered starry night. I did not look back, but had I done so, I would have seen the tears stream down his face and fall upon the Slick Brothers membership card. And that is how it ended.

A slight breeze scented with pine and all the life of summer filled our lungs. The moon had disappeared, finding refuge in the clouds. I glanced to my side, seeing only an obscured outline of his face. "Steve?"

"Yeah?"

The clouds steadily parted and the moon returned to its freedom. We looked into each other's eyes and smiled. "Always."

> **Chris Chambers-Ju,** 18, Redwood City, California

IN THE WOODS

I was concerned about my friend. He had been alone all morning. He walked to our tent around eleven o'clock. The trees in the Sierra Nevadas have a strange way of opening people up.

"Come on," he said. "Let's go on a walk."

I chased after him as he walked into the woods. My friend walked purposefully in his green jacket, but his eyes seemed to pout. Rex, a younger kid, tagged along. He wanted to smoke. We would frequently go deep into the woods to have meaningful conversations and indulge in forbidden cigarettes.

We walked a ways and stopped in a clearing where we sat on a log. My friend lit his last cigarette.

"I'm going to tell you something that I haven't told anyone," he said softly.

His hand began to tremble as he brought the cigarette to his mouth and drew in the blue smoke.

"I'm going to say it fast because it's hard," he murmured as his stoicism was tested by the weight of incipient shame.

I watched him. At that moment the sun on his face made him look more noble than at any other instant in the short time I had known him. Palpable energy was filling his body.

"Promise me you won't think any differently of me," he said.

Rex and I promised. Rex took the cigarette from my friend's fingers and took a shallow drag.

"Eight years ago, I was raped."

A welt burst inside him. Opening up at that instant ruptured a pocket of his shame. I will probably never know the emotion he felt.

I went over to him and hugged him. He put his head on my shoulder and I felt like a father, even though I was a smaller person. Rex stood awkwardly by himself.

"It's OK," he said dumbly. "It's not that bad."

I glared at Rex and he was silent. I don't remember how long my friend shook. After a moment he pushed me away.

"It's OK, Chris," he said. "Eight fucking years." He sighed.

He wiped underneath his eyes. The moment passed and it was as if it had never happened. His voice did not betray him when he said, "This has been the best experience of my life."

I discovered what it meant to be a friend that day. Before, friendship meant hanging around and not saying anything serious. I am grateful and honored that my friend shared this memory with me, despite the fact that it was painful. It is in times of greatest pain that individuals are brought closest. That was the first time I loved a friend. Hearing my friend say that painful sentence has made friendship a word I do not take lightly.

4

First Love

"WHY DON'T WE GO upstairs to my bedroom," she said.

I couldn't believe she was finally ready to do it. While at times, it might have felt as if we'd been together for years, we'd really only been dating for five weeks.

Lynn and I had met through mutual friends at an open house party. From the moment I saw her, I felt an immediate attraction. But it was once we started talking that I knew my feelings went deeper than superficial teenage lust. We, for lack of a better word, "clicked." She was so easy to talk to. I felt comfortable speaking to her about anything. And despite my reputation for being somewhat obnoxious, nothing I ever said seemed to shock her.

The only obstacle standing in the way of our burgeoning romance was the fact that we were enrolled in different high schools. While we lived in the same town, Lynn's parents had sent her to a private school about twenty miles away from the local public school that I was attending. Despite this minor inconvenience, we managed to spend most afternoons together. Once I even cut my last two classes so I could drive to her school and surprise her on her campus with a rose.

I had traveled great distances and made a lot of sacrifices in order to make her happy. I thought I had found my soul mate. Everything was perfect those first five weeks. All our friends thought we made the perfect couple. It's funny how in the world of high school relationships, going out with someone for a few weeks makes you think you know the other person as well as you know your lifelong friends, everything is on fast-forward and you think you've got endless tape.

But back to Lynn's proposition.

"I need to ask you a favor first," she added. "I hope you're OK with it."

Given the circumstances and the critical state of my raging hormones, I felt certain that I'd be OK with just about anything at this moment, *just as long as we had sex.*

Instead of "consummating our young love" for each other in her bedroom, Lynn suggested that we move to her parents' room. Considering the fact that they were out of town for the weekend as well as the comfort of their king-size bed, the request seemed only too reasonable. But it was Lynn's next demand that sent our relationship careening past the bounds of normal teen high jinks and into a dimension so bizarre that I still have no wish to rid it of its mystery.

"I have a present for you," she said. "It's cologne. Do you mind putting it on?"

Things turned odd when she came back with the bottle. It was not gift-wrapped, there was no ribbon or bow attached to the bottle, and there wasn't a box anywhere in sight. Although this slipshod presentation disappointed me at first, I shrugged it off, since my main motivation was decidedly elsewhere. Then, after putting on the cologne, I quickly noticed that the brand was not familiar. But as a seventeen-year-old guy's knowledge of cologne is limited to five different scents, with three of them being from Calvin Klein, the foreign fragrance failed to sound any alarms.

And still, there was something about my new aroma that

bothered me. I couldn't put my finger on it, but it conjured up a nagging feeling of anxiety. Then after about a minute it hit me; not something, but someone. Lynn had asked me to put on her father's cologne.

No sooner had I realized this than I felt a numbness creep over my body—a huge transformation from what I'd been feeling a minute before. There I was lying down on top of Lynn on her father's bed, wearing her father's cologne. I knew that even if I still wanted to have sex, I wouldn't be able to perform due to my shock and horror.

Much as it pained me to jump to any hasty conclusions, I couldn't help wanting to get out of Lynn's house as fast as possible. So I abruptly stopped kissing Lynn and sat up on the bed a good two feet away from her. Then, I told her something I never thought I'd say to a girl in the situation we were in:

"I'm not feeling very well. I think I've got a pretty bad headache."

She just stared at me silently. I could tell she was nervous. The mood was suddenly very awkward. Finally, she turned to me.

"I think it might be better if you leave then," she said.

I didn't need to be asked twice. I slowly got up, put my shirt back on, and headed for the door. She just lay there on the bed staring out the window. I didn't expect her to walk me to the front door. As I was about to leave the bedroom, I heard Lynn say, "I hope your headache gets better."

"Thanks," I said, without turning around. "I think it was the cologne."

All the way home I could not stop thinking how this was the same girl to whom I had given my varsity jacket. The girl I'd had all those feelings for, and yes, they'd been innocent emotions, the type all people have when facing what they think is their first true love. I think Lynn's emotions were a bit more complicated than that.

Although we never spoke about that day in her parents'

bedroom, Lynn and I broke up a few days later. The discovery that Lynn did not fit my image of the ideal girlfriend taught me a valuable lesson about my "ideal." I learned that no matter how pretty, angelic, or otherworldly a girl may seem to be, she is, no doubt, all too human, with the same fears, insecurities, and troubles that I'd tried to avoid, time and again, simply by finding the "perfect" girl.

I needed something to believe in, and at that time in my life, finding that girl seemed like the obvious solution. No matter how impure my thoughts had been, or how seedy my friends' gossip could get, no matter how disgusted with the world I became, it seemed that the right girl, the perfect girl would be able to make everything better, would somehow bring back the innocence I had lost along the way. But as I, like so many others, eventually found out, no one, not even the "perfect" girl has the power to do that.

Even though I'd experienced the pangs of romantic love only too often in my teenage years, I hardly expected to see the same ideals mirrored in the letters of today's teenage boys. Despite having graduated from high school only eight years ago, I somehow allowed the popular misconceptions of teenage boys to infiltrate my own mental schema. The teensploitation movies that have glutted our theaters in recent years all sent the same message, that most guys are out for sex, and that the true romantic is as elusive as a needle in a haystack. I had only to look back at my own experience to realize the fallacy of this sweeping generalization.

Don't get me wrong. Guys are still interested in "getting laid." But if these entries are any indication, they are just as interested in falling in love. That's right, girls are not the only ones who fall in love with the idea of love. The first poem, "Someone to Share," by Ryan Bis, sets the tone for the rest of the chapter by describing the ideal relationship, two souls united by unconditional and selfless love.

This dream of true romance can reduce even the strongest

of adolescent boys to tears. Sure, we've all heard of girls crying their eyes out over an unrequited love, but when Ryan Gardner admits to doing the same in "The Letter," we cannot help feeling a bit surprised. Surely, he must be the exception to the rule. Not according to Zach Reed's "I'm Sorry." A quarterback on his high school's junior varsity football team, Zach is perhaps the last person anyone would expect to see crying over a broken heart. And yet, that is exactly what he does at the thought that he and his girlfriend are now "just friends." Although some might say that the speed with which Zach rebounds from the relationship is indicative of an immature nature, the reality is that he behaves with more civility and decorum than most people twice his age by remaining friends with his ex and making a conscious effort to help her in a time of need.

In the realm of intimacy, it seems that teens are considerably more courageous than their older counterparts. The trend visible in all these letters, and underscored by David Winsor's "Me, Myself and Her," is to aim for an eternal love. Maybe its because as adolescents boys are expected to sow their wild oats that they show no fear of commitment, just an overwhelming desire to fall in love and live happily ever after. For David it's a fairy-tale ending. Whether or not he and the object of his affections will indeed wind up as the high school sweethearts who make it to the altar is uncertain, but as far as David is concerned, his relationship will last forever, if only by virtue of his own intense emotions.

The last selection focuses on the romantic disappointments that add up to create the mature male's somewhat cynical outlook on love.

The anonymous writer of "Go on and Love" presents an all-too-realistic depiction of a teenage romance that's rooted in fear and based upon lies. Since his girlfriend, Mary, looks the part of a dream girl, and he himself is anxious to experience the love described in the opening poem, "Someone to Share," the writer is quick to overlook Mary's flaws along with her infidelity. In the end, the task of keeping the relationship afloat is too great. He chooses to strike out on his own and in so doing sheds many of his illusions about love.

> **Ryan Bis,** 16, Toms River, New Jersey

SOMEONE TO SHARE

The thing that makes me dare
Is that I want a person with me to share.
I wish for love to sit with me,
And to see all I see.
To hold them while watching the other's program,
With our feelings open and not covered by a dam.
Hold her and never let her go as I begin to cry,
And I complement her, never saying good-bye.
She knows everything about me.
Of her I know all that can be.
Nothing is secret, nothing unknown,
All has been said, all has been shown.
To the one I love, to the one I care,
To be with her, to have someone to share.

> **Ryan Gardner,** 15, Castro Valley, California

THE LETTER

The letter arrived two days earlier. He still couldn't open it. He was sitting at his desk staring at the computer screen, but not typing anything. The letter. He couldn't stop thinking about that letter. About her.

It was from her, but he didn't have the guts to open it. He didn't really want to know what she wanted to tell him. He just wouldn't admit that it might be over. That the letter would tell him that she didn't feel the same way. The letter. She had sprayed it with her perfume and the smell was making him crazy. He missed her so much. And even when he wasn't home, near the letter, he could still smell her. On his jacket, on his backpack, and he could taste her kiss. The lips that were covered by cherry lip gloss.

He only wished he could taste those lips again. He would give it all up to go back and be with her again.

But she was gone. And the letter was the only way to know if they would ever be together again. His friends all said she wasn't worth it. That no girl was worth all the tears he shed for her. They said they only wanted him to be happy. But he was always happy with her, he told them, then went home and cried his eyes out.

And he wrote. He wrote whatever he felt. All thoughts in his book. But in writing, nothing had changed. The problems remained the same.

And then the letter came and he was really happy again. But then he thought. He thought what it might say. And was afraid. He didn't want to be lonely anymore. And he didn't want to be sad. He just wanted things to be how they were.

The letter. Glancing down from the screen, he took it and, without thinking, opened it. He expected the worst but only saw a picture. A picture and a note that said "I love you."

And he cried.

> **Zach Reed,** 15, Soquel, California

I'M SORRY

W hen Mary Ann gave me the note at the beginning of biology, I was shocked. I had been doing some last-minute cramming for the big test. When she handed it to me she said, "I'm sorry." I asked her what for but she just walked away. I opened the note, it said:

Dear Zach, I don't think I can be a good girlfriend to you right now. I still like you and everything but I need to work out my problems by myself. I'm so sorry.

Love, Ally

p.s.—If you want to talk about this after lunch we can. If not I understand.

I couldn't believe it. I just sat there with my mouth hanging open. For the past two months Ally and I had been so happy together, or so I thought. I barely managed to get through the test (I just found out that I failed it—55%). Apparently, Mary Ann had read the note and told some people what it said because all of my friends in that class came over and said that they felt bad for me because she dumped me with a note. I thought about that for a while and it made me mad. I told Mary Ann to tell Ally to meet me by the benches in the first quad after lunch. I was still mad when I saw her waiting for me after lunch. But when I saw the look on her face all of my anger just melted away.

"Can we go somewhere else," she said. "I'd rather not cry here."

We walked over to Lyons Park, which is right down the street from my house and the school. She asked me if there was anything specific I wanted to ask her.

"Why?" I said. It was the only question that came to mind.

She started crying. She said that she was having family and personal problems, and that she felt that she needed to face them alone. I said that if we were together, I could help her with them. She said that she didn't want to drag me down with her. I gently lifted up her chin and told her that never, not even once, had I felt like she was dragging me down.

This is where she was supposed to say "I love you" and kiss me, and we were supposed to get back together and live happily ever after, but that only happens in movies.

"I'm sorry" was all she said. The phrase was slowly becoming the motto of the day.

"I just can't give you my all right now and that isn't fair to you," she continued. "There are a lot of girlfriends out there that can be there for you always, like you were always there for me."

"But I don't want any of them. I want you," I protested.

She shook her head. "I'm sorry."

After a lot of tears shed on both our parts, we walked back up to the school and parted for the first time without a kiss. As I lay in bed that night I thought, why now, just three days short of our two-month anniversary? Then the full realization of it hit me. No more weekend-at-the-beach make-out sessions. No more spending our free period at my house talking and kissing and having fun. No more walking her to her classes fishing for a kiss. I admit it, I cried (a little).

The next day at school, I almost started crying when I saw her. We said hi awkwardly. I guess that I expected her to come up to me and say, "I'm sorry, I made a mistake, take me back." But that never happened and I now realize that the chances of that happening were one in a million.

When my ex-girlfriend Crista heard that Ally and I had broken up, she started showing interest in me at school. She even asked me out. But it was too soon for me. Amy and I had only been broken up for one day. I still had way too many feelings for her to go out with anyone else.

Ally and I have been broken up for almost a month now and we are really good friends. We still hang out at our free period but just as friends. I still wear the ring she gave me on a necklace to show that I still have some feelings for her. I am going out with Crista now. After Ally and I broke up, it was Crista who was there for me. She helped me get through the breakup a lot better then I would have gotten through it on my own. Ally says that she is fixing her problems and I am there for her still. I will always have a shoulder for her to cry on.

I have a feeling that when Crista and I break up, Ally will be there for me, like Crista was before. I just hope that when Crista and I break up nobody says, "I'm sorry."

▶**David Winsor,** 16, Ponte Vedra Beach, Florida

ME, MYSELF, AND HER

Me, Myself, and I
That's how it's always been in my life
I've never had someone to hold on to
Like I've got this girl I felt I always knew
She's the one I've been looking for
Since the moment I unlocked the door
To my precious little heart

Never did I think it would come true
What's happening in my life with you know who
She plays with my so-called mind
In a way I think is fine
It only happens when I'm not with her
I unleash my hidden feelings for her
And when I'm close to my love
Those feelings show through my eyes, I am not tough

For that moment anyhow
That I'm holding her so proud
Since I found my one true love

I cry when she's not to be found
Since she's all I want to be around
My life is incomplete without her
I can't believe its so for sure
I'm in love with a girl so grand
She's who I want in the stands
Of the game of my dreams

As I lie myself to sleep
She's all I really want to keep
In my life for eternity
Like a love who will never turn on me
Since I dream of her every night
Holding my pillow so tight
I would just die internally
If she wasn't still with me
When I am old and dying slow
Maybe I will go painlessly
As I lie there in her arms

Me, Myself, and Her
This is what I want for sure
No more me, myself, and I
As I look into her eyes
I see what I need to endure
To devote my life to only her.

> **Anonymous,** 17, Pennsylvania

GO ON AND LOVE

For a while, during my freshman year of high school, I dated this sophomore named Mary. She was an attractive girl, and all my guy friends agreed with me on the important factor that her boobs were big. I met her at church, but our time together at church functions was definitely never very God-centered.

We met at a time when she was insecure and starved for attention. She had broken up only a few months earlier with a guy named Steve whom she'd been going out with all through middle school, and she still felt empty from being dumped so suddenly.

Of course, she had already found a new boyfriend a few months before I met her. But even after she claimed she loved me, it still took her a few weeks to dump his ass. She was real insecure like that.

So she was longing for attention, and I was looking for ways to prove myself independent and capable. We quickly fell in what we thought was love, and got physically involved in no time.

We were both convinced that our relationship was deep and revolved around true love and complete trust, although we'd only met in April and were going together in July, even while she was still technically "going out" with this other guy. Really, we hardly knew each other. I mean, we spent hours on the phone and as much time together as two fifteen-year-olds who can't drive can manage. So we knew each other's life history and thoughts and ideas and hopes and some of each other's fears, but we didn't really *know* each other. I didn't know how she'd react to events in her life, how she really conducted herself, or what she was like if she wasn't your girlfriend. All I knew was that she was pretty fun to talk to, that I was getting a piece, and that she was my first girlfriend and by God our relationship was going to work and last, no matter what my friends said.

The relationship strangled my development often. I traded time that I should have spent getting to know people in the high school or working on my extracurricular commitments for time together with Mary. I'd stay after school to lift weights during the winter, and she'd wait for me, urging me to hurry up and spend time with her when I was done lifting. So I'd do my bench presses, some curls and tricep extensions, a few sets of sit-ups, and leave after maybe a half hour of working out. Then I'd go meet up with Mary and we'd put on our winter jackets and go make out in the baseball dugout.

One time we were in there really going at it—I mean we still had our clothes and coats on and everything, but she was lying on top of me on the bench and we were really smooching—and a guy walked up and said, "This dugout's made for baseball players, not lovers!" I was scared shitless for a moment, thinking it might be a teacher. But then we looked up and saw that it was just an older man who was just going for a walk. He grinned at us, and said before he walked off, "Go on and love."

Mary and I were often touching when we were together—holding hands, putting our arms around each other, kissing. And people often disapproved, especially in school, basically saying we shouldn't do that. But they didn't truly care a whole lot, just as long as she never got pregnant and as long as they didn't have to see us doing much. They'd disapprove, but their attitude was basically, "Go on and love."

After a few months she really cheated on me hard-core, going out with another guy while we were still together. I should have dumped her, but I didn't. I was too dependent on her.

A few months later I was exhausted by the relationship. We were physically intimate, but we were at a line that I wasn't ready to cross, and she wasn't putting forth much energy to build other aspects of our relationship. So I broke up with her, still a virgin.

We once constantly told each other that we couldn't imagine living without the other. We've talked maybe five times since we broke up almost two years ago.

Part 11

Our World

5

School Ties

HIGH SCHOOL is a microcosm of the real world, the strong prey upon the weak, the anonymous both admire and revile the celebrated, and there's never enough time to do everything we want. There is, however, at least one major distinction; everyone is forced to have at least some contact with everyone else. Unlike our lives in the real world, our high school experience bring us face to face with people from every corner of the social spectrum. It is within this framework that we first begin to construct a sense of self.

Trying to decide on what to think of the world around us and figuring out where we fit in sets the tone for the rest of our lives. Whether we believe school to be a battleground as does Tom Meyer, a social fishbowl as does Kyle L. Marquardt, a den of every-man-for-himself apathy as does Christopher Luyt, a warm and friendly place as does Tim Larson, or a realm where we have the opportunity to carve out our very own niche, as does Andrew Zatz, it will no doubt inform our adult hood and the way we perceive people in the "real" world.

Tom Meyer's poem, "Battle Zone," likens the experience of returning from school to that of returning home from the army. As evidenced by the tragedies in Colorado and Arkansas, schools have changed over the years. And although we see the violence that affects our boys on television, we have no idea how it feels to go to school on a daily basis and fear for our lives.

Despite the growing number of violent outbreaks in today's schools, our learning institutions continue to be an important source of knowledge and experience. Going to school is what gives us a sense of self. People may change after they leave high school, but a part of them will always feel like the person they were back in the day. Whether gawky and withdrawn or popular and charming, we will think back to high school and remember it as one of the most important and influential times of our lives.

Although it would seem as if Kyle L. Marquardt's essay "The Play" might have fit in better in chapter 10, on outsiders ("Outside Looking In"), I included it in this chapter to show the amount of social pressure young boys are forced to contend with. Even though Kyle is by no means unpopular and has plenty of friends to call his own, he is ridiculed by his peers for showing up to the play alone. It's an unwritten law of high school life that we do not go anywhere without our friends. If there is so much as a one percent chance that we might wind up sitting alone in a room full of our peers, we are to forgo the night's plans, and remain within the confines of our homes, where we are safe from the certain social death that is the direct result of being seen alone. As ridiculous as this sounds, Kyle's touching account of a night on his own explains why so many of our boys are so anxious about their social standing at their schools.

In the essay "Why Can't We Reach Out," Christopher Luyt points out that in the dog-eat-dog world of school and popularity, it's every man for himself. Relieved that he has his own group of friends, Christopher looks on the less fortunate kids in his school with some pity. He sees them trying to put on a brave face, but is not fooled for a minute. He knows full well how important it is to have a clique, a buffer against the cold, uncaring world, and doesn't want to ruminate on the plight of those who don't fit in. His reaction to the so called "outsiders" is similar to an adult person's confronting someone homeless or mentally ill on the street. We feel bad for them, but unless we are searching for reasons to be grateful for our own lot in life, our fear and general lack of initiative prevents us from taking the time to think about what they are going through.

Although Christopher bemoans his inability to reach out and help his fellow students in need, Tim Larson's story about a moped shows just how compassionate and caring young people can be. When his pride and joy of a moped breaks down, Tim finds that he can't afford to pay for the new engine. That's when his friend suggests mobilizing his peers to help subsidize the cost. After taking up a collection and appealing to the other students' sympathy, Tim gets enough money to fix the moped, proving that young people aren't really apathetic, they just need to feel close to a cause to contribute.

In the best-case scenario, schools can give our boys a sense of security, confidence, and purpose. Andrew Zatz's story is a perfect example of how this works. Faced with the daunting prospect of writing and delivering a speech in front of his class, the awkward young boy rises to the challenge. After making his whole class laugh, he discovers that entertaining his peers comes with its own social rewards. More important, the classroom setting and students help him come to grips with the person he is rather than the person he thought he was.

> **Tom Meyer,** 14, Valhalla, New York

BATTLE ZONE

School is a war, where you go into many situations,
And what's gonna happen? No one knows.

Going to school, like being dropped into a battle zone.
There's allies, there's enemies and then there's always
neutral people.
The allies are your friends, the enemies are the bullies and
the neutral people are the teachers.
Going home is like being released from the army, it's one of
the greatest feelings in the world.

▶**Kyle L. Marquardt,** 16, Cedar Rapids, Iowa

THE PLAY

First off, let me mention that I liked the play. Good acting,
good plot. It was a funny play. Second, I would like to say
that this was an experiment. For the record, it wasn't. I actually
planned for it to work out. You see, I'm a cynical optimist.

It didn't work out.

Honestly, it started out nicely. I walked into the building,
and bought a ticket.

"You can sit wherever you want. Except don't sit on anyone's
lap," said the ticket seller.

"Oh, that would be uncomfortable for everyone involved,"
I said.

Ha. Ha.

I was planning on meeting some friends at the play. When
I walked into the building, I didn't see them. No big deal. They
could be in the theater.

My friends weren't in the theater. No big deal. They had
time.

I sat down in the back row, away from others, hoping that
my friends would see me and sit by me. Five minutes later, the
lights went off and my friends hadn't entered. It was beginning
to feel like a tryout for a bad Woody Allen movie.

Luckily, a couple of friends (not the friends I had expected to see) walked in.

Unluckily, they either didn't notice me or decided not to sit by me.

The friends I had been expecting never showed up. I had been stood up by people I wasn't even going out with. And they weren't women either. I had hit a new low.

I sat back and relaxed. I could talk to friends during intermission and switch seats. Be brave, be suave, be debonair.

I stayed in my seat during the intermission. I'm not suave, I'm not debonair, and I am anything but brave. Instead, I read the back of my program. It involved donating furniture to the Performing Arts. Everyone else got up, but I remained stubbornly glued to my seat.

Sitting two rows in front of me were some people who didn't like me. They pointed at me and laughed a couple of times. I felt like the child molester you always see sitting at the back of elementary school productions. No one came to talk to me. As a paranoid, cynical optimist, I took that as indication that everyone hated me. I slunk down as low as I could in the chair. I saw Dr. Klugman our school principal, give me a sad glance.

I sat, sweating profusely, through the second act. Little did I know there was a third intermission. By then, my paranoia reached a new height. Every conversation, every laugh—they were all about me.

I considered slitting my wrists with my program.

The third act was spent figuring out how I could get out of the theater as quickly as possible. I considered jumping out of my seat immediately after the closing of the curtains and sprinting to my house. But that would not have been practical, considering that my house is about a mile away from the school and I am out of shape. So instead, I made a beeline for the exit to the arcade and hid behind some bushes while I called my dad to pick me up.

When I finished my call, I saw Jerry, our school security guard, pointing at me (I wasn't all that well hidden, it was partial cover at best) and talking to another security guard. I quickly walked out from behind the bushes to avoid a security guard charging me and putting icing on my evening's cake.

It cannot be mentioned enough that I liked the play. The characters were wacky, the plot was very Neil Simon.

> **Christopher Luyt,** 17, Florida

WHY CAN'T WE REACH OUT?

My mother drops me off at the school gate. I wave goodbye and walk into yet another sad story.

Some stand in groups and talk about their exciting weekends. How they went to the "Vaal" with their speedboats and had a really good time. How they worked all night on Friday, but got a good wage.

They laugh together.

Their friendship is special and warm.

As I walk over to my own group of friends (happy to see me), I see others walking side by side sharing with one another . . . and I see those standing alone, looking at their watches, reading through their school diaries. Looking busy.

I know that they are just shielding themselves from the reality that no one is willing to be their friend.

"And me?"

I turn my head and walk on. Much faster than before.

"Got to get to my friends now!"

The bell rings. We go to class. Only to face more mysteriously withdrawn characters. Only, they sit at bigger desks. They are less approachable.

Yet, they have lives too.

Some of them.

After school they climb into their cars and drive off.

But I'll see them again tomorrow . . .
perfectly veneered.

"And me?"

Well, I only have to see them for a few more months. What's more, I have my own veneer to polish.

And yet, when I go home (to my comfort zone), put on my music, and stare out over the hilltops and see the "sophisticated" human anthill from my mansion in "Florida Hills," it hurts . . .

Because I wonder how much I actually care.

"Not much," I say and pick up a magazine on the glass-topped coffee table.

> **Tim Larson,** 18, Fargo, North Dakota

If you happen to attend Fargo South High school around the same time I do, you may have noticed an odd sight in the morning. In almost freezing conditions you may notice a pudgy, goofy-looking kid on board a small, sticker-covered moped with a bright orange flag, traveling speeds not reaching higher then twenty-five mph (downhill with the wind against his back).

Not at all embarrassed, I will admit that the pudgy, goofy-looking kid is myself. It's not that I want to ride that thing when it's freezing but I kinda have this responsibility. It's like this, the moped was kinda the family tradition for a person's first vehicle. This means that there was about a two-year period when I got to drive this two-wheeled monster. My friends would see me on it, I would give them rides, and I was the envy of all junior-highers. After a while I was known as "the kid with the moped."

I wound up riding this thing all the way through high school. The moped was fun and it often made people smile. That was when it happened. On the way to some summer classes the thing came to a sputtering halt. It wouldn't move.

I called my parents and we tossed it into the back of a car. We took it to the auto shop, telling them to fix the problem. Unfortunately we didn't know what the problem was. But hey, it's just a moped, right? Can't be that bad. Finally they finished fixing it and called us. The bill was $240.00. FOR A MOPED!!!

Apparently the engine was shot and they'd had to get a new one. Now I just had to pay. But how?

I was taking classes during this time and had no time to work. I let the problem sit, and sit, and sit. For about four months the problem sat. I basically forgot all about the moped until I got this phone call saying that unless I picked it up soon they were gonna sell it. I was in trouble. I needed an idea.

I was in school and I was asked why I hadn't ridden it to school very much. I explained the story to a friend. He told me that because the moped was so well known I should start a fund. I thought I would give it a try, never thinking it would really work. For a day I carried a jar around school to all my classes. Friends asked what I was doing, and when I told them how I was saving the moped, they had to help, mainly because I was pathetic. After the first day I had made about thirty dollars in change. I thought, hey, let's go all the way with this.

So despite the pleas of my principals, my friends and I made posters and announcements on the intercom and even wheeled a piano out from the choir room to sing a moped song we wrote in between classes. Friends from around school would throw in their change, and by Friday the toll was in. I owed my school big time for the way they helped me out. We had made $260. The moped was saved. We took the extra twenty dollars and got some coffee and tacos.

So now if you happen to see me driving a moped in cold

weather and I don't wave, its not that I'm snotty, just real real cold.

▶ **Andrew T. Zatz,** 17, New City, New York

F or this project you and your partner must prepare a five-minute speech in which you defend your side," my teacher continued. It was social studies class in fifth grade, so I knew who my partner would be: my best friend, Matt McMurphy. The viewpoint Matt and I were assigned to was "The world should be doing more to conserve wheat." Lucky us. We got the relevant topic.

We separated into our groups and began to organize our thoughts, and it wasn't long before I began to drift away from the task at hand to begin doodling, something I had become very adept at doing. I quickly sketched a little comic strip about a talking bale named Mr. Wheat. I showed it to Matt and, as he laughed, he said, "Very funny, but we have to do our speech." My eyes lit up and I ran to my social studies teacher. "Could we do a skit instead?"

When the day came to do our speech, we began to act out the comic; I played the part of the evil farmer and Matt the part of Mr. Wheat. During the scene where Matt was scooting away from me as we both shimmied chairs across the classroom, I fell on the floor with laughter and looked up to find the rest of the class laughing with me. I, who had neither the courage nor the right to talk to my more popular classmates, was suddenly the center of attention. Needless to say, when the class voted, the sanctity of wheat was preserved. I had been given a drug of sorts, attention, and I was instantly addicted.

This little skit I had helped put on revolutionized my life. Standing in front of the classroom and getting applause and laughter was a euphoric experience. As a child, I was extremely shy, quiet, and naïve. This personality didn't seem to be doing wonders for my social life. The Mr. Wheat experience inspired me to nurture another side of myself. I became the class clown. I began to study the timing and presentation of comedians and to emulate them. I would do anything for a laugh. I didn't necessarily do all this to fit in. Mostly, I did it in hopes of repeating the feeling that I got that day in class.

I soon realized that you don't have to be goofing off in front of the class to make them laugh. I can get the same feeling after cracking a good joke while sitting comfortably with a group of close friends or through writing or with comics doodled in my math notebook. Since then, I have successfully been able to merge my timid side with my outgoing side into what I am today, and I often encompass both ends of the spectrum of my personality. But if it wasn't for the gift of humor, I would have never found happiness. In fact, I don't think much happiness really exists without our remarkable ability to make light of things, once in a while, and laugh at ourselves.

6

Toy Soldiers

IF THEY GAVE an award for the least violent high school in the country, I honestly believe my school would win, or at least get an honorable mention. Fights hardly ever broke out, and on the rare occasion that one did, everyone would know about it immediately and it would be big news for a good month.

The students at my school were just not inclined to solve problems through violence. Most probably feared the bad scar they'd receive, that is, on their high school transcript, thus limiting their chances of attending the college of their choice. Also, fights were avoided for fear that the person you hurt might have a lawyer for a father, and you might end up not having the money to attend the college of your choice. My town had a lot of lawyers. Someone was always suing someone else, don't ask me why.

But while my classmates pretty much stayed out of trouble, I can still recall a time during my senior year when I was forced to live in fear. An innocuous comment I made to the wrong person resulted in a grave state of affairs for myself as well as my close group of friends.

Due to the segregated social climate of my high school, jealousy and resentment were running rampant among social cliques. Although these attitudes were rarely expressed verbally, let alone physically, I have to admit that there was an undercurrent of tension among certain groups of students. Even though my circle of friends was generally well thought of, I soon found out that none of us was without natural enemies, enemies that if pushed too far had the potential to strike back violently. I found this out the hard way.

They were called the "Brewster Roadies." They attained this appellation by hanging out and smoking cigarettes on the road in front of the school when they should have been in class. They were a toned-down version of the stereotypical "bad kids" that no school can exist without.

My friends and I were oblivious to them. We never interacted with them and if they showed up at a party we were throwing, they were always denied entrance. We never thought of the repercussions of our behavior.

This all changed one day when a friend of mine bumped into one of these so called "roadies" in a hallway. A fiery exchange of words erupted, largely instigated by the guy my friend bumped into. It was as if he was unloading four years of animosity toward us in that hallway. He ended his verbal assault with a threat of violence, just before a teacher broke up the potential fight. Believing ourselves to be impervious, my friends and I paid no attention to his threat and went on our carefree way. This was easy to do, since ignoring the "roadies" was a matter of course.

Despite what happened that day in the hallway, the next couple of weeks at school were uneventful. It wasn't until I ran into a couple of friends at the town library that things took a turn for the worse. They asked me how things were going and we started talking. For some reason, during the conversation I thought it would be funny to tell them the story of the hallway altercation. I told them how ridiculous the roadie was and how he threatened that he and his friends were going to "smash our faces in." They suggested that I should pay someone to kick his ass first, just in case he was serious. Thinking they were joking, I agreed and said that I would definitely take their advice. Little did I know that one of the guys I'd been speaking to was actually a cousin of the roadie that my friend had bumped into. Word of this chat would soon get back to the Brewster Roadies, who, for their part, would fail to see the humor in my remark.

The following weekend my friends and I hosted one of our usual keg parties. Everything was going great right up until the moment we heard the loud sound of breaking glass and cries for help coming from the driveway. When we all ran outside to see what had happened, I found my friend Josh lying next to his car, which had the front windshield smashed in. As I helped him to his feet, I saw that he'd been badly hurt, he was covered with blood. I immediatly yelled for someone to call an ambulance.

I knew right away who Josh's attackers were, and Josh confirmed my worst suspicions the next day, when a bunch of friends and I went to visit him at the hospital. He told me that the roadies weren't done and that they were going to systematically "take care" of each of us. When I suggested to Josh that he should press charges, he refused, saying that it would only cause more trouble. For the next four weeks I lived my life in constant fear, terrified that my name was next on their list.

Living in fear is something many boys have learned to deal with. Reports of school shootings, security checks, and metal detectors are par for the course. Just another day in the life of an average teenage boy. Although I had felt sorry for myself for having to live under the threat of violence, my experience was nothing compared to the current situation in our schools.

The essays I have chosen for this chapter all deal with some form of violence and aggression. Whether it's a video game that's gone too far or a prank gone awry, these stories of frustration and anger reveal just how dangerous our school climate has become. And while high levels of aggression have long been associated with teenage boys, it is clear that something has to be done in order to provide boys with new outlets for their pent-up rage.

Upon reading Blair Williams's "The War," I couldn't help but recognize myself in the narrative. Like Blair, I, too, had gotten in plenty of hot water because of my big mouth. In my naïveté, I never expected that words could hurt just as much, if not more, than punches.

While some boys fight fire with fire, others simply choose to walk away from violent confrontations. Such is the case with Matthew Richter, who writes about trying to control his anger during a basketball game. After being shoved to the ground by his opponent, Matthew thinks about retaliating but opts not to fight.

The next two pieces reveal some of the influences responsible for violence. Dave Bove's descriptive poem "Tabletop Commander" shows the powerful impact video games can have. In describing his strategy and the trajectory of the game in full detail, he reveals that video games have gone beyond mere entertainment. His serious tone and obsessive description show that the line between fantasy and reality is growing fainter every day.

Ryan Armstrong's story "A Lesson for Mr. Perry" depicts a group of friends trying to exact revenge on a teacher for punishing their best friend. The writer has qualms about egging the teacher's house but, encouraged to act aggressively by his friends, he goes along with the plan anyway. When the teacher suffers from a heart attack the following year, the narrator must come to terms with the shame of having harmed a weak and defenseless old man.

I chose to place the poem by Richard Jackson last because I felt it to be the most graphic example of what violent thoughts can do to a boy's mind. When I read the verses detailing the slaying of the narrator's family, I was shocked by its gruesome depiction and strong imagery. Fortunately, the teacher who sent in the poem assured me that the young man has a handle on his anger. More promising still is the poem's ending, which indicates that Richard can indeed see well beyond his violent impulses.

> **Blair Williams,** 18, Tallahassee, Florida

THE WAR

If there is one thing I can't resist, it's getting attention from everyone around me. I'm one of those people that have a comment for everything, and if I can't think of a comment, I'll do something that will get me the well-deserved attention I require. It was my loud mouth and immature antics that finally made me realize one of the most sacred rules ever set by man: "Do unto others as you wish they would do unto you." I learned this rule in the seventh grade on a cold winter's day, a day that changed my life, and taught me to think before I speak or suffer the consequences.

It all started on the bus one day after school. At the time I was hanging out with a group of kids who apparently thought they were better than everyone else. These guys were much bigger than I was, but thanks to the funny remarks I made about other people, I was soon accepted into their clique. The boys lived in my neighborhood, so every day after school we would jump on one of their trampolines or play tackle football in the backyard of our so-called ringleader's house. As time went on, my funny remarks turned to outright insults, and then one day I insulted the wrong person. He was in eighth grade at the time, and he accidentally heard me talking behind his back. He turned around and told me to shut up. Embarrassed in front of my friends, I snapped back, "Why don't you make me, queer." This little comment dug me a hole I would never be able to crawl out of. This little comment dug me a hole that I would soon be buried in.

The war was on. Every day on the bus I would shout to this little eighth grader, but he never said a word back to me. I used everything in my arsenal: jokes about his mom, jokes about his dad; I even made fun of his grandma. He would always shake his head and continue the conversation with his friend on the bus. At the time I felt proud of myself because every time he did this, my friends would laugh and would urge me to say something else.

At this immature stage of my life, I would have done anything to get a good laugh, so I kept pouring out the insults like I was looking for the prize in the bottom of a cereal box. Finally, I crossed the line. One day as I exited the bus, I accidentally hit his head with my elbow. He stood up and said, "You just wait; you'll get what's coming to you." In the back of the bus I could hear my friends laughing, so instead of saying I was sorry, I gave him a fake laugh and got off the bus. Hours later we were playing a good game of tackle football on my friend's trampoline when the two boys arrived on their fixed-up Trek mountain bikes. It was the eighth grader I had been tearing down with my insults and his friend from the bus. He told me to meet him at the top of the hill, and if I didn't show, then I was a chicken. Suddenly I wished I had never made fun of this little eighth grader who all of sudden seemed larger than life. My two friends urged me to go, and said if I got in any trouble they would rescue me. I believed them and made my way to my black Schwinn ten-speed and started up the hill. Nothing could prepare me for what happened next.

I reached the top of the hill and parked my bike in a grassy field with my two bodyguards at my side. As I looked around, I saw nobody except my two excited friends. A grin appeared on my face, and I said, "Look, the chicken didn't even show up." Suddenly I heard the sound of gravel under a tire. It wasn't loud enough to be a car, and that only meant one thing: The chicken had arrived. I started to get that sick feeling in my stomach, the kind you usually get the first day of school or the first time you take a girl out. His head slowly appeared as he climbed the hill to the battlefield. His face was filled with disgust, and fear suddenly filled my body as I watched him dismount his bike. It was at this point in time that I realized I was in big trouble.

I was waiting for the usual middle school fight to erupt. First, there would be a shoulder-bumping contest, followed by a bunch of trash talk. Second, a push fight would commence, and then it would eventually develop into a fistfight that is usually broken up after a couple of punches are thrown. Unfortunately, this fight was nothing like that at all.

As he approached me, I waited for our shoulders to meet. Standing with my hands at my sides, I received a walloping blow to the nose that knocked me back a couple of feet. I was in shock; I had never been punched before, and I had no idea what to do after being punched. Finally I came to my senses and attempted to throw a punch myself. It probably resembled a wounded duck more than a punch. I missed him completely, and then received another punch to the eye. That one really hurt, and my retaliation consisted of hugging him, trying to wrestle him to the ground. He then threw me to the ground and pinned my shoulders down with his knees. He asked if I had had enough. Instead of saying yes, I continued to run my big mouth. As he rained blows down upon me, my two friends just watched in pity. Suddenly, I had an epiphany; if I had never said anything in the first place, then I would still be playing that wonderful game of tackle football instead of being pounded into the ground. Finally I gave in, and the massacre ended. My two friends just watched me in dismay as I mounted my bike and made my way home.

Christopher Harrison had taught me a lesson I will never

forget. His lesson stuck with me physically for three weeks; this is how long it took my two black eyes and the other bruises on my face to heal. His lesson has been glued to me emotionally for the past six years. Ever since that fateful day, I haven't made fun of people who talk, dress, or even look different from me. It is not my place to tell someone how to dress or how to act. I take people for who they are because people accept me for who I am. I guess you could say that I got some sense knocked into me.

> **Matthew Richter,** 14, Elk Grove, California

I stand alone wrapped in sweat
And the heat of my anger
My normal calm, kind attitude
Is decimated by a stranger

We play a game with a hoop and a ball
We play it with reasonable skill
His shots go in as much as mine
Why must he be a pill?

For he shoots and he makes
And he celebrates
I drive back down hard and I score too
He decides he must retaliate
"He cannot do as well as me!"
He thinks in utter disgust
So he shoves me to the ground
Because he feels he must

Does he feel it is wrong for someone else
To be as strong as he?

Can others not be able and fit?
Will he lose some dignity?

I could understand if he were in loser land
And always felt beat
But he does as well as me legally
Why does he feel he must cheat?

These questions burn through my mind
And I almost dare deliver a smack
But I think of how I felt and then
Quietly turn my back.

> **Dave Bove,** 17, Ocean, New Jersey

TABLETOP COMMANDER

Knee-deep in death, I wade across the battlefield
The air is filled with smoke and the moans of the dying
Floating in the sky, I take in everything below me
The battle's fury has taken its toll on the land
The once green fields now blackened and scarred
My troops have been forced back into defense positions
The enemy is making a strong advance
My mind is lost in thought, I'm there, yet not there
Viewing from afar before taking action
The hurried assault is crushed
The hasty general tastes defeat
I'm cautioning myself
"Take your time"
When my concentration is shattered
I hear "Are you gonna move?" ring out from the sky
And I look up, into the face of the enemy

The slightly glazed eyes, framed by glasses
The chubby face covered in a patchy beard
I look down and realize I'm in the real world again
There is only a bunch of painted models on green felt
Dice and rulers strewn across the board
Not what you'd call great war host
But I have my secret weapon
Step back
Take a good look
Then act
A sharp grin spreads across my face
And as I look into the eyes of the enemy
I can see the beginnings of fear
I'm in control again
I will reach out my hand to touch the world
This will change everything

> **Ryan Armstrong,** 15, Aurora, Colorado

A LESSON FOR MR. PERRY

We rode bicycles through the unlit suburban street without Sam that night. Brad, Rusty, Kevin, and I rode as swiftly and as gingerly as we could. Kevin was hauling the ammo he had bought from the grocery store earlier that day. Kevin rode ahead of us with his anxious feet kicking at the spinning pedals of his bike. I could see the marks of fear in his body language. His hands grasped the handlebars so tight that they were turning bright red. His hair was pouring with sweat as he stared straight ahead.

No one talked on the way there. I presume all of us were flooding over with nervousness, even Brad. I could never picture Brad being panicky. His toughness and proportions would brush anything fearful off. When I looked behind me, I saw his eyes swelling with dismay. I smirked to myself and peeped over to Rusty, who was also laughing at Brad's expressions. It felt good to get out a laugh. The thing was . . . we didn't stop. Brad and I just couldn't stop and we carried on all the way down Savannah Street.

Eventually we all started laughing, even Kevin. His feet still thrusting the pedals with much anticipation. The laughter faded after a moment as we went back to the silence of night. My hands became sweaty upon the handlebars. I pulled them down and stroked off the darkness onto my ebony sweater.

I've never done anything like this before. I didn't know how to act in this queer situation. Should I exude the toughness that Brad always shows or be more cautious like Kevin. It really didn't matter as we struggled up a hill. Our purpose was just a few streets down as the night was at rest and absence of light overtook it. My heart began beating rapidly as my bike came over the hill.

The gang stopped and stared.

"This is it, no one talk from here on out. Got it?" Brad barked.

We all nodded except for Kevin. I know he was thinking about his brother at home, Sam, who was grounded for just about the rest of his life. Maybe I'm exaggerating. At least a good part of his teenage existence. Brad's eyes glanced over at Lenny as he repeated himself, "Got it?"

Nothing.

"Got it, Kevin?"

"Yeah, I got it," Kevin pronounced finally.

"Ease up a little, Kev, We'll be out of here in a few minutes," Brad said trying to calm down Kevin a bit.

"Yeah, Kevin. Just wait until your brother hears about this. He'll friggin' die laughing, dude," I added to Brad's words.

"All right, all right! Let's do this, damn it," Kevin stopped us. He sped down the hill, not even hesitating for us. I groaned and flew after him. I knew his rage was waiting to be let out. Not only did he hate Mr. Perry but his brother was caught by him too. Sam wasn't the one who had pulled the fire alarm, but since he was the only kid around and because of his dire reputation, he was the one blamed. Sam was expelled from school without any proof of his crime. Sam wasn't the greatest guy in the world, but he was our friend. Actually, he was my best friend.

The whole ordeal led us to this. It was Brad's idea. The gang just agreed. Kevin, of course, being the last one to subject to this payback. Kevin wasn't exactly the wild child of the family (I'm pretty sure Sam received those genes). Neither was I for that matter, but Kevin was really a mellow kid.

I saw Mr. Perry's house. The roof was missing many shingles and the house was badly painted. Large chips of crumbling paint were visible in the darkness. The front door couldn't be seen; an expiring maple tree blocked my view. The grass was long and growing onto the sidewalk. Flowerpots sat at the end of the driveway. The flowers that filled them were long dead.

Brad broke the silence as he proclaimed, "Everyone take three. Hit it fast so we can get the hell outta here." His hand held the carton open as we each took our own amount. Brad then took the big one out and handed it to Kevin. It's stench took the air around us abruptly. I pulled my nose away and coughed.

"C'mon. Brad and I will go up the front. You and Rusty get the sides. Make it fast," Kevin ordered as he and Brad began moving. Rusty ran up the driveway while I stood on my bike just staring at the shoddy-looking house.

The first egg hit hard across the front window. Brad threw all of his next, which splattered across the front door. Rusty threw his at the garage and ran toward his bike like a crazy man. Kevin hesitated and then threw the bag at Mr. Perry's front door.

Kevin, Brad, and Rusty rode away as the light above the

front door went on. It burst open to reveal Mr. Perry in his checkered underwear and a bathrobe. He began to shout something but I wasn't able to make it out. I couldn't believe what we'd done. All I saw was a withered old man standing before the door. His hair in a flurry, his knobby legs barely able to help him stand, and his beady eyes starring into the blackness through his tiny glasses.

I dropped my eggs and began to catch up with the others. They were waiting for me at the top of the hill. We rode to Brad's house and spent the rest of the night laughing about the mission. I didn't laugh as much as the others. Honestly, I didn't know what to think.

A year has passed since our adventure that night. I haven't talked to Brad in a long time and Rusty moved a few months ago. That's OK with me. I'll miss both of them. Who knows, maybe I'll get back together with them in the future. Whatever.

Kevin and I are still friends. He hasn't changed much. Still the anti–wild child.

Mr. Perry died the winter after we egged his house. His heart attack shocked the whole school. It was odd. At that point our gang began to dismember. I can't remember if I ever threw those eggs. Whether I dropped them or they had hit the house it doesn't really matter. Not anymore. To this day I wonder if he ever got the stench out of his door.

> **Richard Jackson,** Congers, New York

A
TINY
DROP
OF BLOOD
DRIPS SLOWLY
OFF THE KNIFE OF
THE SERIAL KILLER, ON
THE FLOOR NOTHING BUT
RED, NOT A SOUND IN THE AIR
FOR THEY ARE ALL DEAD, NO MORE
FIGHTS ON CHRISTMAS, NO MORE BITCHING
ABOUT THE FOOD, 'CAUSE I KILLED THEM ALL,
LIKE THE VOICES SAID I SHOULD, WITH THE
BLOOD ON THE WALLS AND ALL OVER
MY FACE, I NEVER STOPPED TO
THINK HOW TO GET OUT
OF THIS PLACE.

7

Free to Be

THROUGHOUT MY CHILDHOOD, I always knew exactly what it was that I wanted to do with my life. I wanted to be a doctor like my father. Even when I was too young to understand what he did, I could see the respect and admiration he inspired in others. At that point, I didn't care about what he did so much as the fact that I wanted to be just like him when I grew up.

When I finally grasped what my father did for a living, my motivation was not deterred. In fact, I could hardly wait to start following in his footsteps. It didn't even matter that he was away from home so much of the time. I was determined to have everything he had: pride in his work, respect from his peers, and a happy, fulfilling family life. At the time, I thought all doctors were instantly granted these things along with their diplomas.

The more I studied in school and applied myself, the prouder I felt. I thought I was that much closer to becoming more like him, and that was always my main goal. Through high school and even college, I worked hard to get good grades. I never once questioned my decision to become a doctor. I had sworn to become an M.D. and would die trying.

Needless to say, I didn't become a doctor. But I didn't abandon my desire to help others either. I was still planning to involve myself in the health profession and pursue a Ph.D. in psychology, but something about my desire to become a medical doctor had waned. I soon realized that it wasn't so much being a doctor that interested me, as much as being more like my father.

When I discovered this about myself, I felt as if a huge weight had been lifted. I realized that I had been pushing myself to achieve something I really had no interest in. It was that precise moment that marked my entry into manhood. I had made a decision that had nothing to do with my parents' or society's expectations. I had asserted my independence once and for all.

Nowadays, when I meet a young boy, I always wonder about what it is he wants to be. Used to be we all wanted to be firefighters or police officers. But no longer. Saddled with more expectations than ever before, today's young men seem as if they'd come out of the womb with a burning desire to pursue careers in law, medicine, and high finance.

But expectations don't only come in the form of career choices. Emotional and behavioral expectations and misconceptions are still keeping our boys from fully realizing their potential. Told to suck it up and keep a stiff upper lip, boys often forget what it is they want in order to please their parents, peers, and teachers. So how do young boys break free from the limited image society has of them? How do they find the courage and strength to follow their voice and ignore the millions of others clamoring for their attention?

The essays in this chapter all have to do with our struggle to find our own unique voices and identities. All of the entries illuminate the difficulty of keeping up a persona that is either false or worn thin.

The touching and familiar theme running through Jason Longo's "Reflections on the Yards" took me back to the first time I began to question the path of my own life. In describing a summer job working on a boat, Jason illuminates many of the expectations that have plagued his youth. Having taken for granted that he would try for good grades and go to college, Jason first envisions the existence of an alternate path while he is working on the ship. Imagining all the freedom he would have sailing the open seas, he finally comes to accept that what he really wants to do, what he's dreamed of since he was a little kid, is a fantasy made unattainable by his conventional, upper-middle-class upbringing. When the summer ends, Jason returns to the real world of school and college applications, leaving his epiphany on the ship where he found it.

Our curtailed freedom to do exactly as we wish extends to the act of crying. There have been plenty of times when I wanted to cry, and I would have too, but for the fact that I felt as if I was somehow breaking a male code of honor. Daniel J. Klotz's piece, "Vulnerable," addresses this common male misconception. Taught to sublimate feelings of vulnerability and weakness, Daniel finds himself in the awkward position of wanting to cry. But when his mother interrupts his reverie, he treats the event as a close call, and rebukes himself for the momentary lapse in judgment.

In Kevin Naber's composition we see a much more defiant tone. Whereas the former piece showed a resignation to fulfilling the predetermined roles, this essay introduces a young man actively defying all those influences that threaten to limit, define, and misrepresent him.

The next two selections address the issue of what it means to be a man. To some, it means playing sports and acting macho. But according to Kyle Jones's poem "Two Worlds," being male and playing sports don't always go hand in hand. Preferring the creative outlet of poetry to the violence and blind aggression of sports, Kyle decides to do as he pleases, even if it means going against the grain.

Reinforcing the message of this last poem is the narrative by Brent Garrett. In describing a drill sergeant's violent attack on a new recruit, the author likens the brutal confrontation to the football game going on a few yards away. His purpose is to show that pressuring young boys to match the stereotypes of jocks or soldiers can have dire consequences.

Finally, Drew Bennett's essay "A Giraffe Is What I Want to Be" really sums up the difficulty that all boys must eventually overcome. In this well-written and profound story, Drew explains that growing up is little more than discovering all the things we cannot do.

> **Jason Longo,** 17, Manhasset, New York

REFLECTIONS ON THE YARDS

"They must think I'm crazy," I thought as the cable I was standing on swayed back and forth under the yard with the wind, the rocking of the ship and the movement of the person working on the port side of the yard with me. I was wearing only a T-shirt and shorts, but the wind was cold, and the sun, already low in the sky, was covered by the clouds. I looked at the crew member working in front of me, and I saw he was dressed the same as me, except he was barefoot.

"At least I'm not as crazy as him," I thought to myself, as I continued to help furl the main topsail, more than sixty feet above the surface of the ocean. I strained, leaning over the yard on my stomach, pulling up on the heavy canvas of the sail. I had a safety belt that was clipped onto another wire running along the yard, but it looked like it would do no good if my feet slipped off the cable.

"You finished out there?" my companion called. He had finished before me.

"Just finishing up this last knot," I called out, my words being tossed out behind me by a gust of wind.

"I'm going over to the other side to help them out. Can't have women doing men's work like furling tops'ls." He grinned at his joke. "You could go back down to the deck, or just hang out here for a bit, and take it all in."

I peered down at the deck, and watched the others standing or walking around in pants and jackets. I then looked due west, at the horizon, and watched the sun slowly set. The clouds stopped just short of the horizon, and I watched the deep orange sun in a thin patch of sky between the clouds and the shoreline. The clouds looked beautiful, in hues of purples and blues, and the ocean a deep, dark blue. To the northeast, a squall line was moving toward us, and I could see the fall of the rain, a dark purple against the clouds, even though it was at least a half hour away. I realized how dark it was, and I felt at peace that Wednesday. Then I had a sudden thought.

When one of the crew called out for volunteers to help furl the sails, I had immediately grabbed a harness and climbed up the ratlines. Going up, I thought I knew who I was. I was a kid with one year of high school left. I had to think about grades, and colleges and what I wanted to do with myself for the next fifty or so years. I wanted to have a good job with good money, a house, and a car. At least that is what I thought I wanted for sure when I climbed up into the rigging that evening.

I had never thought about skipping college and traveling around like a free spirit, or getting some bizarre or insane job that I would enjoy doing just for the hell of it or because it was interesting. The only time something like that came to mind was when I would bug my mom when she asked me about colleges or my future. I told her I would join the French foreign legion or work as an Alaskan crab fisherman or something bizarre like that, but only for the reaction. I would always get some face from her that I thought was hilarious, followed by either a sigh, a shaking of the head, a "What the hell is wrong with you?" look, or a lecture about why would I throw away all I had going for me. I had rarely thought about college, and even now, with less than three months for me to write and send out my applications, I still had trouble making myself care enough to think about it.

I had only sailed on a tall ship to see what it's like to sail on a square-rigged ship, and to live out a dream I had since I was four. My dream had evolved even further than I thought. Now, as I stood, stretching my knees and watching the sun sink over the horizon, with the lights of towns and houses blinking in the deepening darkness, my wandering, free-spirited self wanted to live like this. I loved traveling, the ocean, sailing, and historical and strange things. As I stood there, I realized college didn't really give me any of those things. I would do something I really loved even if it paid little, its skills applied almost nowhere else in the world, and it was different from everything else. Doing something that paid well, having skills that were useful, and being part of a respected profession doesn't appeal to me if I don't love doing it. I turned around and saw that they were almost done on the other side of the yard, and I began to climb down to avoid the rush. As I climbed down, I cursed myself for watching one of the most beautiful sunsets I had seen and not having the chance to snap a few pictures of it. The last of the sails were furled, and I wasn't needed on deck anymore. I went down to my bunk to relax and read a little. I was comfortable and hoped that the call of "All hands on deck!" wouldn't force me to leave my bunk.

With the book lying on my chest, I thought about what I really wanted. I was confused. One part of me wanted to have a good, normal job, and a good education, and the other wanted me to do something outrageously fun for my life, and to hell with money and education and stability. I was a little bothered by the fact that these thoughts were coming out so late in my life. I was frightened by these crazy, conflicting thoughts flying around in my head, colliding like atoms with an explosive force.

I still don't know what I want to do. I'm applying to colleges, and obviously still in school. I figured those thoughts just came out because it was summer, and everything I did that summer was different from what I'd done every other summer in my life. I had a lot of new experiences, and my mind had been opened to all sorts of new things. Those free-spirited thoughts still exist though. They still collide with everything I am doing now, but they seem to have been subdued or pushed to the far corner of my mind. If they are going to stay there, I do not know.

I untied the last knot on the starboard side of the fore top-gallant yard. The sail fell from the yard, and hung in the bunt-lines and the other lines that control the sail.

"ON DECK!" I yelled from more than one hundred feet up in the air.

"Deck on!" was the faint reply.

"Fore t'gallant is loose and in its gear!" I yelled. I heard an answer and I stood up to take a look around me. I could see for miles around me. I looked at the tangled web of lines and cables below me. I saw people walking on the deck, or just milling around. They looked so small from where I was. I saw the bow wave of the ship as it sailed along, soon to be under all nine of its square sails and a number of its staysails.

I think about that now, and I realize something else. Though that was all a new experience for me, I felt oddly at home, and comfortable. Like I had been doing it for a while, even though I was just learning it. Perhaps I was home, being a wanderer, going wherever the wind took me.

> **Daniel J. Klotz,** 17, Jacobus, Pennsylvania

VULNERABLE

Tonight I was truly vulnerable, for the first time in years now that I think about it. I was taught at an early age that it is OK for boys, even men, to cry and be "sensitive." However, that was a lesson that I was told, and real life, of course, argued it.

So I was in a bit of a dangerous position, really, in that I knew I really should not cry, but I felt a strong impulse to. If I had been seen, it would have appeared to the observer that I was crying over an argument I had just finished having with my mom over my decision not to baby-sit this evening. It would appear that I had lost control over a silly little thing.

In truth, however, I found myself crying for quite a different reason. I had just watched a very powerful film earlier that afternoon, a moving love story in which hundreds of innocents died. The experience of watching this intense movie had already put me into quite a reflective mood, a sort of melancholy, passive, almost lonely mood. Then, this argument with my mom, although minor, pushed me beyond the bounds of my own emotional control.

After the argument, I began thinking about a friend of mine who killed himself last year at the age of fifteen when he drove off in a truck and shot himself because he didn't have any real hope. Then I thought about another friend who died a while before that when the 747 he was riding to France with his foreign language class crashed into the Atlantic off the coast of Long Island. I thought about his family, which included one of my best friends, and how they're still dealing with the grief, and how they never found out what caused the tragedy. And I thought about all the kids who starved to death today.

Seeing that I was alone, I allowed myself to cry for a minute or two before I got up to leave and set the table for dinner.

Just as I opened the door, my mom was reaching to come in from the adjoining room. Usually things like that don't faze me. I know people who would get startled, and others who would be scared, but usually I take a surprise like that in stride.

But this time I reacted unusually, drawing a quick, decisive breath and jerking back. Immediately realizing how vulnerable I had been to be so startled, I sighed in disgust and quickly walked out of the room, chastising myself for allowing my hard shell to come off.

▶ **Kevin Naber,** 16, Fort Wayne, Indiana

FEELINGS, BELIEFS

To those who would rather impose their own personal beliefs on me than give me a few short minutes to figure things out for myself . . .

I Ignore You.

To those who would give me those minutes, only to mock me and hate me for what I might come to believe . . .

I Don't Like You.

To those who would hear what I have to say, but still believe it to be wrong because it doesn't conform to what they have been told all their lives.

I Pity You.

To those who would take my words to heart, accepting (but not necessarily understanding) that this is what I am . . .

Thank You.

> **Kyle Jones,** 14, California

TWO WORLDS

Sports
Poetry
Two worlds I delve into daily
Two worlds so different from each other
It hurts to have both exist
Pain
Sweat
And Death
Lie in the running
The push-ups
The sprawls
Poetry mocks this world
With its cynical eye
Why take pride
In this degradation
Why conform
To the sadism
Of naïve teammates
In my poetic stage
I say what I want
I tell my emotions
Of pain
Suffering
And Love
That society has conditioned males not to say
Sports reinforce
Society's view
To make males "tough"
When all that happens
Is the self-mutilation
Of guys

I know very well
This self-mutilation
I choose poetry
Over the impending death
That sports reinforce

▶ **Brent Garrett,** 18, Rougemont, North Carolina.

ASSUMPTIONS MAKE . . .

D emetrii had never been this hot before, had never known this kind of heat. His helmet felt like an oven under this hot southern Arizona sun. Why was he even here, he wondered to himself. No one had ever asked him if he wanted to be there. It was just *assumed* that this was his calling. Demetrii had a very good feeling that that word would be his end one day . . . assumed.

But whining would do him no good, for here he stood, among all the other lemmings, it was too late for him now. Demetrii looked around and saw that everyone else was just like him. Young, strong, full of life; they hadn't volunteered, but they sure had some proud fathers. Little boys scared stiff trying to do exactly what they're told.

"Do you have a problem, boy?" the drill sergeant bellowed directly into Demetrii's ear. What was he supposed to answer? He knew whatever he said would result in a hard fist to the jaw, or maybe this time it would be to the stomach.

"Sir! No, sir!" Demetrii screamed out, just like he'd been taught.

"Are you saying I'm an idiot, you pitiful maggot!? Are you saying I'm BLIND! Apparently you didn't hear the question correctly. Do you have a problem, son!"

"Sir! Yes! Sir!" Demetrii screamed, trying to hide his anxious fear.

"That's what I thought, you maggot. Now, it's good to seee you can admit when you're wrong," the drill sergeant smiled like a king who knows he's got complete control over his subject.

"Now, get on your knees," demanded the drill sergeant. Demetrii closed his eyes, clenched his fists, and did what he was told. The drill sergeant took his size-six-and-a-half shoe and, like the football player he'd never been, punted Demetrii across the training yard. He didn't stop until Demetrii was a bloody curl on the ground.

One of Demetrii's friends ran to him even though he wasn't supposed to. Everyone said that those two looked just alike, with their leather-colored hair, and all those freckles made them almost look like brothers.

"Oh my God! Sir, you killed him."

"Impossible! Get up, private . . . I said get up, private!" The drill sergeant stood and waited. The longer he stood in the quiet of the scared boys the more it sunk in, what he had done.

"I was just doing my job. I'm supposed to be hard on you all . . . I thought it would be good for him . . . he was too weak."

The drill sergeant got on his knees and stared at his hands as if something was on them.

Across the street from the army base at the high school a team of Pee-Wee League football players were busting themselves trying to make their coaches real proud of them.

> **Drew Bennett,** 18, Colorado Springs, Colorado

A GIRAFFE IS WHAT I WANT TO BE

There once was a smart little boy, and he loved to dream and wonder. His parents told him he could be anything he wanted to be; they told him he was special, even though he was no different than you and me.

But the boy was young and did not know about the world and so he said, "I do not know what I want to be."

Then one day the little boy went to the zoo. He saw many animals there and he said, "This I know is true, I do not want to be caged like a tiger, I want to live wild and free, yes this I know, this is what I want to be." And then the boy learned of a place called Africa, where the giraffes lived wild and free. "Oh, yes," the little boy said, "this place is very much for me."

So the little boy went home and told his parents, "Oh, a giraffe, a giraffe is what I want to be."

But his parents only laughed, "Oh, you fool," they said. "A giraffe is not human like you and me. No, no, a giraffe you cannot be."

The little boy was sad and confused because he did not know what they must mean. For his parents told him he could be anything that he wanted to be.

And so time passed and the boy did not know what to be. Until one day he went to school and he learned about our great country. "A founding father," he said. "A founding father I want to be. I want to fight against greed and tyranny. I want to fight for justice, peace, and liberty. Oh, a founding father I want to be."

And so he went home and told his parents, "Thomas Jefferson, Thomas Jefferson I want to be." But his parents laughed and said, "You can't parent a great country. Look around you. Can't you see, we are already so very, very free. No, no, Thomas Jefferson you cannot be."

And the little boy was puzzled, for he did not know what they must mean. For his parents told him he could be anything he wanted to be.

So much time did pass, and the little boy struggled to find what he wanted to be. And then one day he said, "I am a smart little boy, this much I do know. I can teach many things. I can help people's minds to grow."

So the little boy ran home and shouted out with glee, "Mom and Dad, come and listen to me. A teacher, a teacher I want to be."

But the little boy's parents only smiled and said, "A teacher is a very difficult thing to be. You do not make much money. It's hard to live so happily. No, no, a teacher you do not want to be."

And the little boy was sad again, and did not know what to think. For he was always told, he could be anything he wanted to be. But now he knew there was something more, something he was supposed to be. And so he asked his parents, "What then, what should I be?" And his parents smiled and said, "How about a doctor or a lawyer, they're great things to be."

Then the little boy looked down at his feet, and a tear fell from his eye. And he thought to himself, "Oh, I do not know, I do not know why."

Sadness filled the little boy's heart, then he looked at his parents and said, "OK, OK, a doctor or a lawyer is what I must be."

Much time did pass and the little boy became a man, and he had a child of his own. He told him he could be anything he wanted to be.

Then one day his little boy said, "Oh, an elephant, an elephant is what I want to be."

And the man laughed and said, "Silly boy, silly boy, an elephant is not human like you and me. No, no, an elephant you cannot be."

8

Escaping into Oblivion

THE GAME is called chandeliers. The objective, as with all games of its kind, is simple: to get as drunk as possible. The optimum number of players is about four to eight. The only requirement for participation is that all players must share a burning desire to drink beer, and lots of it.

Basically, chandeliers is a more sophisticated variation on the classic drinking game "quarters," where a quarter is bounced off a table with the aim of sinking it into a designated drinking glass. When a player accomplishes this goal, he or she earns the right to force any other player present to drink. I won't get into the details of chandeliers, except to say that it elevates quarters to a binge-drinking art form.

My friends and I played this game almost every weekend during high school. We all loved it. That is, until the incident with Andy occurred.

Andy was one of my best friends in high school. We, along with four other guys, were inseparable when it came to weekend parties in our town. We never missed an opportunity to either throw a party or attend one. Andy's parents were out of town at least one weekend a month, so his place was the perfect spot for the quintessential "keg" party. All week long Andy would rave about how much fun the upcoming party would be.

"I'm gonna get wasted," he'd boast, high-fiving anyone who shared his enthusiasm.

Back then I never thought of this behavior as unusual or a cause for alarm. Everything we did seemed so normal. Only the "bad" kids used drugs, but everyone drank. I remember that people would get smashed and eventually vomit, only to say "tank's empty now, so give me another drink." Of course, if we ever saw the same behavior exhibited by adults, we wouldn't have thought twice about labeling them alcoholics. But we were teenagers, and according to all the movies and TV shows we'd ever seen, only old, homeless, and unkempt men could be alcoholics, not young, good-looking, and athletic high school students. I guess we were kind of naïve. No one ever questioned the status quo in high school—for most people that process starts sometime in college—but for me, it was the night I took Andy to the hospital.

Through the din of the music and the roaring party crowd, I could still tell something was bothering Andy that night. He was too serious, too quiet. His motions around the table seemed almost robotic. I had never seen him like that before. We were playing for about two hours when Andy left the table, saying that he was going to go mingle in another room. We'd hardly noticed his departure, so engrossed were we in the action.

About twenty minutes later I had to take a bathroom break. I didn't want to relinquish my seat at the table but since I'd been off my game all night, I really had no choice in the matter. When I got to the bathroom, I had trouble opening the door. Once I managed to pry it open, I couldn't believe my eyes. There was Andy, Mr. High Tolerance, lying on the floor, passed out cold. I remember shaking him, asking him if he was OK, but there was no response.

I had never been so scared in my life. Andy's face was as

white as a sheet. His eyes had rolled back into his head. I barely remember what happened next. I guess I must have called for help, because a handful of people rushed into the bathroom. I remember that one girl kept saying, "Oh my god" over and over, but no one knew what to do. Finally, I pulled myself together and told someone to call an ambulance. But even as I barked out the orders, I couldn't quite grasp what was happening.

It was only under the glare of the bright hospital lights that I was able to come to grips with the situation. Andy was OK. The doctors pumped his stomach, and as I sat waiting for his release, I thanked god that my friend was going to be fine.

When I drove him home from the hospital, it was already four in the morning. My parents wouldn't be up this late. Usually I'm glad that my parents trust me enough not to wait up for my arrival, but this time I wished that I could talk to someone about what had happened. I tried to sleep, but all I could see was Andy's ashen face. "What if he had died?" I thought, and all because of a stupid game.

A stupid game that I had taught them. It had started innocently enough. I thought back to the first day I showed my friends how to play. I felt like such a big shot. Everyone was looking at me with a mixture of interest and admiration. I was introducing them to something new, something exciting. Now, all I could think about was that I was responsible for Andy's collapse. I had initiated playing the game. I was accountable.

I spent all of the next day on the phone with Andy. He said that he would never drink again. But when the next weekend rolled around, he was at it again. Although he'd sworn off chandeliers, game or no game, Andy was still chugging beer as if nothing had ever happened. No matter what I did or said, Andy like so many of my other friends would continue drinking as before. As far as I was concerned, however, drinking had taken on a whole new meaning. From that day forward, I abstained from the binges that had once defined my weekends.

Guys in college would sometimes give me a hard time, calling
me a "lightweight" for not finishing off my beers or for refusing
to pull a beer bong, but I just think of Andy's sickly face and
prone body lying on that cold bathroom tile, and say, "whatever."

The horrifying memory of Andy's accident came back to
haunt me when I read "Toxic Shock." Like me, the author
learned a terrible lesson. Rushed to the hospital after consum-
ing too much alcohol, Armando discovers that drinking alcohol, like taking drugs, can have graver consequences than he
ever imagined.

I had always been aware of the phrase "peer pressure," but
like most teens, I never thought that it applied to me. I had
always considered myself somewhat of a leader. But the more
I thought about the role I played in Andy's collapse, the more
I realized that my decision to introduce the group to the game
was incited by my desire to seem cool in front of my peers.

The essay "No Laughing Matter," by Chris Shmader, ana-
lyzes how peers help form boys' attitudes about drugs and alcohol. When his two friends return from a trip with wild tales
about drinking, Chris and the rest of the group laugh along
good-naturedly. While he by no means approves of their behavior, he doesn't want to be a killjoy. Although Chris suspends
judgment, his friend Abe chooses not to feign interest in the
story. Abe is forthright about his opinions, opting to stay silent
during his friends' raucous anecdote. In the end, Chris begins
to admire Abe's approach. He wants to be more like him, but
finds that the pressure of fitting in is too great.

Ryan's dark and somber poem "Ashes to Ashes" leaves the
reader with few illusions about the all too real threat that drugs
pose to young people. The poem begins as Ryan watches his
brother go through different stages of drug abuse. He is aware
of how harmful the effects of the substances are, but succumbs
anyway. This poem demonstrates just how powerful the influ-

ence of others can be in contributing to a substance abuse problem.

In Noah Furman's fictional diary of a habit formed, he reveals the ease with which any upstanding teen can be led astray. In this case, friends are again identified as contributors to drug addiction. In October, the narrator finds himself walking the straight and narrow. He is proud of himself for not trying drugs, and is convinced that he will never try it. But things quickly change when he meets a new transfer student. He is not pressured into trying marijuana, but becomes curious about its effects. Seeing his friends smoking weed leads him to try it once. But one time soon turns into a daily event. Even after his mother discovers drugs in his jacket, the character is unrepentant. The only lesson he learns is that he should be more careful about hiding his stash.

The harrowing quality of Matt Meacham's essay on drugs and sports comes from the adroit way in which he shows the pervasiveness of drugs in every area of a young boy's life. Trying to keep himself out of trouble, Matt involves himself in sports and discovers that he is never completely immune from peer pressure. Watching his friends smoke and drink before games, Matt finds himself on the sidelines, watching his teammates make a mockery of the sport he loves.

Dealing with young people with substance abuse problems is difficult, but nothing is quite as difficult as breaking the cycle of abuse once it's started. The poem "Cain," by Adam Gower, paints a disturbing picture of drug abuse and its victim. Unable to break free from the addiction, the boy in the poem warns others to avoid following in his footsteps.

The next two essays, by Anonymous and Ryan Frazier, are undoubtedly two of the most heartbreaking stories I have ever read. I couldn't imagine someone so young having to go through something so horrible. In "Recycled Minds," the anonymous speaker opens up about his own drug use and the death of his girlfriend. Although terrifying and tragic, his girlfriend's death helped him turn his own life around for the better.

In "My Perfect Wish," Ryan G. Frazier also comes to grips with an unspeakable tragedy, extracting a lesson that he will never forget. He recalls the good times he and his girlfriend shared. Simple things like listening to music and talking late into the night with her was all it took to make him happy. Everything was going fine until his girlfriend had too much to drink one night and got killed in a drunk-driving accident. Ryan expresses his grief openly. He does not try to lay blame, but wishes that his girlfriend's parents would have taken more time to spell out the dangerous effects of alcohol. Even though they had always tried to get her to turn down her music, Ryan claims that they ignored the one issue that really mattered.

> **Armando Fragoso,** 14, Douglas, Arizona

TOXIC SHOCK

I am a regular pretty average kid. Not too popular nor unpopular. I have noticed most all of my friends are similar to me, meaning that they're concerned about school and about having fun. We all pretty much know right from wrong. I do both right and wrong things. Most of the wrong decisions I make are simply because of peer pressure or I simply think, "I'll have fun," "I won't get caught," and "Others always do this, nothing will go wrong if I do it." The situation in which I think these things is when there is alcohol at a party or something similar to this setting. But one time, everything went wrong. It was at a girl's fifteenth-birthday party. At first I thought this party was going to be the same as any regular weekend party. I started out by receiving a beer from a friend. I then accepted a couple more. I started to feel like the party was dead, and to have more fun, I kept drinking more. I started to drink hard liquor, I had tasted it before and not liked it but once I was already buzzed off of beer it just tasted like liquid breathmints, and it went down smooth and fast. All I remember is walking like a guy with a bum leg, in other words almost falling, to an alley close to the party with some guys that had a bottle of something. I could hardly even remember that. The next thing I remember is waking up in the hospital with tubes going in me through everywhere. My mom was in the room crying while the nurse was lecturing me about drinking. I remember understanding her clearly but now I don't know what she told me. Then after they took off all the needles and tubes through which they pumped my stomach empty, I remember the nurse taking me out to my dad's car in a wheelchair. I cried when my parents were driving me home from the hospital because I was thinking, "How could I have done this to my parents. They are the only two people I love more than myself and I, their son, have just made their life a painful nightmare." It felt like I wasn't supposed to be a part of my family for this. I thought about what kind of person my nine-year-old brother and eight-year-old sister were going to think I was. That night, on the trip from the hospital to my house, I felt nothing but guilt and regret like never before. The next morning I didn't want to wake up to face my parents. I woke up and just lay in my bed until my mom came in. She didn't seem mad so much as sad. She said that she and my dad had talked and they felt they couldn't trust me anymore. My eyes started to tear again. All I hoped was that they felt the same amount of love toward me still. She kept talking to me and said my dad didn't even want to talk to me at the moment. She told me they still loved me and that my little brother and sister didn't find out about it because they were sleeping at the time I came home.

She explained to me what had happened that she knows of. I was at a friend's house at around 1:00 A.M. when my friend's dad called my mom to tell her the condition I was in. My mom then picked me up, took me to the hospital, called my dad out of work, and watched as I was being taken care of at the hospital. She said I was resisting the nurses when they tried to put needles in me. I was cursing at them and I was acting like someone else. My mom said it reminded her of *The Exorcist* because that wasn't me at all. She felt she didn't know me. So that's the part of what happened that I was positive of because my mom wouldn't lie to me. The part of the story I'm not positive of is what happened after I came back from the alley to the party. My friend said I was falling down all over the place and everyone went to go look at me and some other drunk guys. (They were drunk too but not as bad as me.) He said him and some more of my friends took me away from the people at the party because all they were doing was laughing at me. My friends took me to a park close to there and just held me up for a while, until I finished throwing up, and then laid me down. I passed out like eight times. That's what my friend said. They got scared for me and they just took me to another friend's house. That's when my friend's dad called my mom and told her. This is what my friends said happened, but I don't remember a second of it. Maybe this *is* what really happened. Maybe they left out a lot of things. I guess I'll never know.

I know it's no one else's fault but mine that this happened. I am the one that swallowed the alcohol. No one forced it down my throat but me. I thank God I have caring friends and loving parents, without them I probably wouldn't be here today.

I would like to say to every young adult that they should think about how much their life is worth, not just to them but to their friends and family, before they take the risk of getting hurt, hurting someone, or even dying by drinking for the sake of having fun. There are a lot more ways to have fun without using drugs or alcohol.

> **Chris Schmader,** 17, Hillsborough, North Carolina

NO LAUGHING MATTER

M ost Friday nights, my friends and I get together and go
to a restaurant, a football game, or the movies. I remember one Friday when we all decided to go to the Lone Star
Steak House near South Square Mall to eat. I was irritated because I was nearly broke and we were going to eat at an expensive restaurant. We all met at the restaurant, and after an
extensive wait near the smoky bar, we sat down to order.

I sat beside my friend Abe. I've always liked Abe because he
doesn't let his peers or even his closest friends change his morals, a rare characteristic for a teenager to have. Everyone at
the table ordered their food (I ordered an eleven-ounce steak
with a sweet potato and a salad, and boy, was it delicious).
While we waited for the molasses-slow service to bring our
meals, we began to exchange stories about what we had done
over the summer.

Two of my friends, Pete and Jeff had gone to a town in
South Carolina together a couple of weeks before school
started. They had gone with Jeff's father and grandparents,
who were apparently some outrageous relatives. Pete related a
tale about how he and Jeff were caught drinking beer on a
sidewalk by a cop who tried to be the tough guy. The two girls
they'd been with had whimpered pitifully about getting in trouble, and Jeff's father reacted with disbelief when he found out
("What the hell were you thinking?!?") The story was hilarious.
Pete and Jeff had not been arrested, so even though I did not
approve of high school students drinking on sidewalks, I still
laughed hard at the way Pete retold the story.

Actually, by the end of the story, everyone at the table was
cracking up except Abe. A very religious person, he sat staring
down at his plate, slowly poking his food. Every once in a while
he would shake his head from side to side. I would never do

what Pete and Jeff had done, but I still thought the story was funny. Maybe I should not have laughed; maybe I was encouraging their behavior. As for Abe, he just kept shaking his head, a solitary pillar at a table of friends whose morals did not match his own.

> **Ryan,** 17, Chowchilla, California

ASHES TO ASHES

Tick, tock counts the clock
As my brother inhales that fatal blue smoke
Tick, tock counts the clock
While my brother guzzles that sweet burgundy liquor
Tick, tock counts the clock
Oblivious to my brother snorting that snowy white powder
Tick, tock counts the clock
Presiding over my brother's painful moaning
Ding, dong chime the church bells
As the holy man preaches ashes to ashes
Tick, tock counts the clock
As I inhale that fatal blue smoke
Ding, dong . . .

> **Noah Furman,** 15, Evanston, Illinois

JOURNALING AN ADDICTION
(*A Fictitious Account*)

October 19: Dear Diary, today a lecturer came to school to talk about drugs. It was the usual sob story about how pot had screwed him for life but he rehabbed and no one should ever do it. My friends and I made fun of the speaker but it made me kind of proud to be straight-edge. I mean, it's not like I haven't had the opportunity. Hell, I get offers every day. Weed is everywhere. The preppies, the skaters, the ghettos, the nerds all do it. It's not like I take offense at them using, but it's just not my style. I've got no desire to. I mean, who wants to screw up now? I'm only a sophomore. Anyway, I've got no need to do it. None.

December 5: Dear Diary, today I met this kid Doug. He transferred to our school a few days ago. He's pretty cool, I hung out with him at the park for a while. After about a half hour of chillin' there he lit up a blunt. I didn't think he smoked weed. He just didn't seem like a stoner. At first I was kind of nervous about cops or someone else seeing us, but it was pretty secluded. He asked me if I wanted a hit, and I said no. It was cool with him, so I just went home. I had work to do, and who wants to watch somebody else get blown? Afterward I worried if my parents would be able to smell the residue on my jacket, so I put it in my closet. I thought about how easy it would be to sneak pot into my house.

December 13: Dear Diary, today I tried weed. It really wasn't that big a deal. Me and Doug and some other dude went to the park. They both smoked up and I asked for a hit. Doug wasn't gonna give me one at first, but I insisted. I don't know why I wanted to. Whatever. It was kinda weird, feeling that first deep breath of it. I've never even tried cigarettes before, so my lungs kinda sputtered a little. Doug and the dude laughed. I was expecting to, like, hallucinate or something, but it was really nothing. I don't know if I'll do it again. My friend Joe offered me a nickel bag a little while ago, so I might take him up on it.

January 7: Haven't written in a while. Me and Doug and Joe have been hanging out a lot more, and I've been stoned a lot more. Hell, the only reason I'm not smashed now is I ran out of money. I cleaned out my mom's wallet a week ago, so I'm waiting for a little while so she doesn't get suspicious. Man, weed is expensive! I gotta go do homework now. I'm like failing half my friggin' classes. Can't concentrate.

January 25: Dear Diary, I don't know why I'm writing this. My mom found a dime bag in my jacket today. I'm in crap up to my neck. I don't know how my dad's going to react, since he's out of town, but I'm sweating my ass off. Doug says not to worry, that he's been busted before, and it's no big deal. Well, I don't have his luck, or his slack-off parents. His mom probably smokes his stash when she gets mad at him. My parents are going to kill me. I'm already grounded for a month by my mom. Next time I'll know not to leave my jacket in the front hall.

> **Matt Meacham,** 16, Suburb in the Northeast

THE WRONG TEAM

I have been playing sports since I was a little kid. In elementary school, my teammates were my close friends. We all hung out with each other and had a blast. Then came junior high. Everything changed so rapidly. We all broke off into our own separate little groups. Some made wise decisions but most fell prey to peer pressure by the "cooler kids." This peer pressure led these people straight to alcohol and drug use. Now that they're "cool," they actually brag about it. In the locker room, they will gloat about how they went to a party the night before and smoked cigarettes, or pot, or took acid or shrooms. Sometimes, even I can't believe it. These kids, the same people that I was friends with in elementary school, show up at practices and even games high or tripping.

Every year we're faced with the sad task of picking captains in each sport. Our standards have to be very low. The person must be able to show a little leadership, he must be dedicated enough to show up at practices most of the time, instead of smoking and who knows what the hell else, and he must be able to stay eligible, whether it is grade-wise or not getting caught with drugs and alcohol.

In the little town that I live in, there are a lot of athletically talented kids. The problem is our teams never have a full roster. There is always at least one prima donna that gets caught with drugs or doesn't do their work at school, probably because they aren't sober, and gets ineligible. As a player, I can't believe my eyes. On the bus ride home from an away game, players are sitting in the back either dipping or smoking. At home games, they walk out the side door of the building and light one up. I wonder about their intelligence. I wonder if they are too addicted to whatever they are smoking, too stupid to realize they will get caught, or if they really just don't care.

In our town, we as athletes have to sign a contract at the beginning of each season that says we will not drink alcohol and do drugs. Attached to this contract is a list of consequences if you do get caught. These consequences are a load of crap and a big joke to the athletes because when the athletes do get caught, the athletic committee always gives them another chance. You are especially safe if you have a popular last name or are friends with one of the athletic committee members' kids.

Athletics has turned from fun and excitement to just politics.

> **Adam Gower,** 17, Buford, Georgia

CAIN

It's coming and it won't stop
Turning you blind

And dropping you from the top.
Don't hit the white train
It will take you out of your game
And put invincible messages in your brain.
It's OK.
Hit the track only one time
It's only one line
After that your mind will shine.
Got you wanting more and more
After blowing your mind
It will have you begging to the Lord.
It came and you couldn't stop
Turned you blind
And took you off the top.

> **Anonymous,** 16, City in the Southeast

RECYCLED MINDS

It has taken me almost three years to finally quit my drug abuse. The addiction can be two different obstacles to overcome, one mental, the other physical. And no matter how hard I try, I still get the feeling, the urge to start using it again. But let me tell you this. When you have overcome those feelings to an extent, it will feel like you have just got the gold medal at the Olympic Games.

My life experiences have given me many reasons to quit. I have had four friends die by overdosing. Another three were murdered over something as inconsequential as a bad deal. Two more were lost to a fatal car accident.

I was about thirteen years old when I started using drugs like pot and LSD. I had smoked cigarettes ever since I was nine; by the time I was fourteen, I was smoking two packs a day (give or take a few). I lived in a rich community throughout my middle school years and half of my high school days. If I hadn't moved when I did I probably would have been six feet under with no visitors.

When I turned fourteen my friend asked me if I wanted to cruise with him and his girl. I accepted because my parents were in one of those fighting moods. When things went flying around that was my cue to leave. Seth and his girlfriend were about fifteen minutes away from my house and this is how the story goes . . . Seth was smoking a joint, driving with one hand below the wheel. His girlfriend was laughing and just all-around giddy. Seth took a turn a little too sharply and spun out of control at fifty-five mph, he crashed into a pine on his girlfriend's side and she flew out the window and died on impact. At least that is what the police told me. While all this happened Seth tried to get out of the car (another thing that the police told me) but was stuck and died from inhaling the leaking gas fumes too deeply. I visited their graves weekly, they had been going out for two years. I always get the most upset when I think about Seth's girlfriend, she had a 4.3 grade point average and a week after her death she was accepted into Brown University . . . So I was told.

About a year later I earned the name "eight ball" by being the only one in my group of friends to survive an overdose of cocaine and weed combined, which is nicknamed "eight ball." Another two of my friends had done it, but they weren't so lucky.

The next thing that had happened changed my outlook on things permanently. I was at my home listening to a little music when the phone rang. It was a Wednesday at 11:00 P.M. This guy named Jay called me, panting and breathing heavily. I was about to hang up, thinking it was a prank call. But just as I was about to hang up the phone I heard him call out the name Tom, who was one of my best friends that I had kept over the years. I listened to what Jay had to say (he told me that he was

Tom's brother). The only thing that I could make out from Jay's panting voice was that Tom had been shot over a bag of speed and fifteen dollars cash. I asked where they were, but I got no answer. The next day I found out that Jay had died, and the reason for his heavy breathing was that he'd been shot in the kidney and bled to death on the ground behind a privately owned grocery store. I still wonder to this day why he called, maybe it was the last request of Tom to have his brother give me a call. It might have been that they were telling me who murdered them but didn't have enough time.

After all that, I just stopped cold turkey with drugs, everything from weed to cocaine; and in the later months I had never felt better. It took a lot for me to quit. One, because it was too hard for me to do it in my mind. And another reason was I was going through the most depressive moments in my whole life.

I had been clean for almost three months when the unthinkable happened. Just another thing to add to my depression. My girlfriend, Jane, and I went to a party to celebrate our anniversary. I was smoking a cigarette when it happened . . . we had been there for about two hours and I was just about to get Jane and leave. I excused myself from some people sitting around swapping stories about their "drug episodes." I walked into the living room, which was right next to the room I was in. That's when I saw her lying there. Her friends told me that she had passed out drunk, but when I lifted her up from off the ground and rolled her over all I could see was blood dripping down her face like a river. She was already dead but I still yelled her name at the top of my lungs so she would hopefully wake up. The guy that was running the party said we all had to leave because he had called the police and an ambulance. He told us to leave now and he would take the consequences with the police. That was the last time I had seen her, except for the occasional visit at the cemetery. Her parents still don't know that I had gone out with her. . . . They never will. As for the guy running the party, he got a two-year sentence for one count of manslaughter.

Now that I have moved away from those dark days I have indulged myself in reading philosophy and history of all sorts. I am on honor roll and have an impressive GPA, I have changed my life by 180 degrees and am proud of it. I still remember the bad times and I know that I will never forget them.

▶**Ryan G. Frazier,** 17, Whitman, Massachussetts

MY PERFECT WISH

I REMEMBER how the sun would hit her face when we'd sit outside on those long autumn afternoons. How she'd just look so deeply into my eyes and whisper "I love you." But that was then, and this is now. Time took her, and there was no way that I could have ever gotten her back no matter how I tried.

The doctors and her parents told me that it was the music that had taken her in, but the doctors and her parents were wrong. She used to tell me that I was her prince, and I used to tell her that she was my princess. We didn't have a care in the world. Not a care.

After sitting outside we'd go back to her house, and go to her room. We'd listen to music for hours, it seemed. Pink Floyd, and Led Zeppelin, and even sometimes, just for nostalgia, Elvis. The music grasped her sometimes, and she'd dance. God, Heaven's angels must have watched her when she danced because she looked so beautiful and perfect.

I used to call her my perfect wish. She was everything that I'd ever looked for in anyone. She was my lover, my best friend, and my hero. But now she's gone. Sometimes I sit alone in my bed and just think "I wish she was here." One of those times is right now.

Her parents used to yell at her, and tell her, "That music will make you go crazy." They always had the time to take away her music, but never had time to tell her that alcohol can be bad. So now she's gone. Another wasted teen life.

I was supposed to go driving with her, but I didn't because her breath smelled like vodka. I should have tried to stop her. I should have held her and made her safe. But I didn't. And now she'll never look so beautiful dancing again. My perfect wish is broken. My perfect wish is broken . . .

9

Outside Looking In

MINE HAS NOT always been an exemplary life, but I can honestly say that I have never made fun of those who couldn't defend themselves. Sadly, these people made easy targets for anyone carrying a chip on their shoulder and looking to blow off some steam. I remember registering the faces of some of the disenfranchised as my friends tried to pick them apart. Few ever really got angry. Most simply walked away. They looked beaten and defeated, and I always felt bad for them.

Of course, I would never have gone so far as to defend them. I, too, had my popularity to consider. But I never once initiated or joined in the ridicule that characterized my school's social environment. The rule at school seemed to be make fun of someone, before someone makes fun of you.

Although I never ridiculed anyone, I always pitied the outsiders at my school, seeing them as less capable and less fortunate than the rest of us. But after reading the essays sent in from teenage boys, I realized that I had been right to abstain from hurting people, but wrong to feel pity. Looking over the submissions, I discovered that many of the outsiders had more courage and perseverance than I had at that age. Their ability to endure in the face of so much opposition makes them stronger and more capable of dealing with conflict later in life. To this very day, I try to keep the peace with my family and friends sometimes at my own expense, a behavior my popularity reinforced in high school.

These boys, on the other hand, will become that much more capable of solving problems and getting what they want out of life. They have learned to be on their own, and are not forced to fit a predetermined mold. We all remember them in high school. They were the quiet ones, the ones whom no one really got to know. But with graduation will come major changes. The social order of high school will cease to exist and only the strongest people will emerge from the clutter. If I had to bet on who would be the most successful in life, I would bet on all of those outsiders at my school. They are the survivors, and will no doubt go on to accomplish great things.

The first letter, "Flying into the Stars," by Michael McAvoy, illustrates how escape into a fantasy life can protect young men from the pain of the everyday. In the essay, Michael addresses the issue of his homosexuality. Although he had suspected he was gay for two years, the realization only dawns upon him one night when he is alone in his room. The fact that other kids ignore and taunt him weighs heavily upon him, but he is thankful for the stars and his rich imagination for saving him from feeling the pain of being different.

We are all different in one way or another. What distinguishes us is the extent to which our differences are visible to the outside world. In Brian Marion's case his difference comes from the neurological disorders ADHD and Tourette's syndrome. As a child, his hyperactivity earned him many friends, but as he grows older, he finds that fewer and fewer people are attracted to his personality. Fortunately, he has his studies and books to distract him. He explains that his studies and reading have helped counter the negative effects of being an outsider.

A marked determination to stay true to himself runs

throughout Brian's narrative. The next essay, by Jeremiah Bingham, reflects an equal level of self-awareness, and demands the same of others. According to Jeremiah, labels are an easy way to classify those who are different; but, as many of the essays in this book demonstrate, they are also responsible for the social alienation and torment of millions of outsiders.

The next two essays display the different perspectives of two teens who are in the same boat. Both Matt Tupps and Brad Oberlander are new kids at the same school. But while Matt remarks upon the strange ways of the natives and looks forward to investigating further, Brad's curiosity is immediately discouraged by the disparaging remarks of his would-be classmates. With their objective view of our subjective high school experience, these perennial outsiders, the New Kids at School, can equip us with a great wealth of insight into our behavior.

The last entry, "A Note and a Scar," by Ryan Kelley, is more than just a story, it is a wake-up call to all the bullies, victims, and parents and educators who are content with an order established upon fear and denial. While underscoring the point that the outcasts can see those who belong for who they truly are, as opposed to who they are trying to be, Ryan's tragic tale posits that it is for this very reason that the outsiders are destined never to fit in.

> **Michael McAvoy,** 18, Madison, Connecticut

FLYING INTO THE STARS

Quietly, my hands gripped the cold wooden rungs of the ladder. It was old and rotting and bent slightly beneath my weight. On my right, a pine tree rose and reached over my head, its branches heavy with a huge mass of intertwined vines.

As I reached the top of the ladder, I hoisted myself onto

the roof and crawled just beneath the cluster of vines. I stood up when I was clear and walked to the center of the roof. It slanted slightly, but was easy to walk on, and not as steep as the main roof from which it protruded, with the old brick chimney.

Just between the two flat skylights in the middle of the roof, I stopped and stared out. The cool dark sky glimmered clearly with stars scattered about like tiny gems; the moon rose, casting a white glow over my yard and the tops of the trees. The only sounds were my dog stirring restlessly chained up in his area, distant cars on the faraway main roads, and an occasional car passing on my street. Every once in while, a jet slowly rumbled across the sky, its green and red lights moving amidst the stars.

I lay down on the cold shingles and let my imagination wander into the night sky. I dreamed of Falcore the Luck Dragon swooping down from away in the distance and bearing me away on his back to the Ivory tower in the land of *The Neverending Story*. I pictured spaceships from *Star Wars* battling overhead in orbit, and I hoped for Han Solo to drop by in the Millennium Falcon to tell me that he needed to take me away to fight some battle against the evil empire. All of these images captured me and took me away.

It was my sister who taught me to climb up to the roof to look at the stars and escape. A long time ago, she used to sneak out and lie on the roof to meditate. She was away now, and loneliness drove me to go to the rooftop, where I could think in peace.

I hadn't many friends at the time, and being in middle school made me feel as if I was trapped among a bunch of people who didn't know me, but judged me. I would sit quietly in class with all of these people around me, and I knew that they thought they were better than I was and that I was unattractive. There was nothing I wanted to do more than to escape, to fly away to a safe magical land.

Not many people bothered me particularly, but no one really paid close attention to me either, and I knew it was because I was gay. Somehow, everything that I hated about myself was due to the fact that I was gay. My funny nose, my acne, the annoying way I talked, my lack of coordination, were all due to my homosexuality, and I was sure that everyone was aware of it.

I would sit quietly as my teacher spoke, not really listening to what she was saying. I usually sat in the back. The desks were stiff and uncomfortable and seemed restraining. I observed the faces of all of the other students in the class. There were always at least one or two guys in the class who I thought were attractive, with their toned bodies and deep middle school voices. I knew none of them were gay. There were also pretty girls in the class, with perfect hair and nice clothes. None of them paid attention to me either. Not one single guy or girl in the class knew me, and still many of them judged me. I knew that it was because I was gay.

When I came to this realization, it was a Sunday night, and I had just finished watching the sequel to *The Neverending Story*. I lay on the top bunk of my bed staring at the tiny screen of my little black-and-white television. Outside, the sun was setting, and the only light in my room was the blue glow of the TV and the warm yellow light from the Christmas candle standing in my window. At the end of the movie, the end title song came on as the credits rolled and brought back memories from my childhood. I was reminded of times when all that mattered to me was fantasy and fun. Relationships didn't matter, and I never felt completely guilty or bad about myself. Seeing *The Neverending Story* reminded me how much everything in my life had changed. Although I had known for two years that I was gay, I hadn't accepted it as my way of life until that night. I sneaked out that evening and lay down again on the shingles. I started to cry. I wanted nothing more than to leave behind this world and go off to Fantasia with Bastian, Falcore, and Atreju, who I knew would not judge me. I looked into the sky and hoped that one of them would come to rescue me.

Now I return to the roof and remember that night. I lie down and stare into the mysterious expanse of stars, and drift away into lands of fantasy. I no longer feel so bad about my life, or myself. Instead I am thankful. I am thankful to have had this place to come to escape, to take me away when I needed, and fill my head with dreams of hope and adventure. I now look up into the quiet shimmering stars and realize how they have saved me.

> **Brian Marion,** 16, Niskayuna, New York

MY LIFE IN 3,000 WORDS OR LESS

My life has never been easy; not for me, and not for those around me. I suppose you could say I was born to suffer—or at least that's how it seemed, when I lost oxygen for a few minutes during delivery. We think that this may have caused the brain damage leading to the mental disorders that have haunted my life like a dim specter, hovering in the corners of my eyes, always herding my life down terrible new paths. It didn't get easier after that; although I was happy much of the time, my infancy was tainted by a crippling case of asthma, a painful and terrifying disease. I can only vaguely recall the sudden attacks; the sudden, familiar clenching in my chest, running desperately to a bathroom to inhale steam from a burning shower, frantic rushes to emergency rooms, and always, always the pain, the fear, the anguish of never knowing when the next attack might come.

The asthma receded gradually, and was almost gone by the time I entered grade school, but it had left its mark: permanent damage to my lungs, making it almost impossible for me to play with my friends for very long without having to stop and sit to breathe. But even though my physical pain was over, it was of little comfort, for it wasn't long after that the other children started settling down and maturing a little. I didn't.

It was hard for me to realize the problem, although everyone else did soon enough. I had been an extremely rambunctious infant, always running around, picking things up, making a mess. Everyone expected me to settle down as I got older. Unfortunately, I never did; if anything, I became worse. I always talked in class, and never paid attention to the teacher; I was constantly trying to talk, to play with other kids, even when they were busy; I was always weird, hyperactive, and awkward. As time passed, the other kids stopped liking me; the same qualities of playfulness and energy that had made me so popular in kindergarten started turning against me. But it didn't stop there. In fact, that was when it started getting worse.

The ticking began. In retrospect, I know that I had ADHD and Tourette's, and that I could have taken medication at any time and led a happy, normal life. But at the time, it was hard, it didn't make any sense. I started getting feelings in my throat, my eyes, my fingers, feelings that felt like a cross between having an itch and having to sneeze, and both a thousand times worse. I eventually realized that I could make the maddening sensations go away, at least temporarily; all I had to do was "tic," a simple word which for me encompassed an amazing array of horrifying behavior. At first, it was mostly motor tics: tapping my finger, flexing or kicking my legs, and eventually, moving into my face, making me blink my eyes, bite my lips, or grimace like some horrible prepubescent gargoyle. Soon, though, the itching moved into my throat, and I found that I needed to start making noises, little grunting noises in the back of my throat, wispy noises using my tongue and cheeks, even clucking my tongue. The pressure to tic became worse when I was bored, and for me, that was every day at school. You see, I was a genius—I understood and remembered everything the teacher said, I always finished my work way ahead of time, and I understood the points my teachers were making halfway into their lectures. So I always ended up in a desk in the corner of the room, tapping my fingers and kicking my feet, trying hard not to make the terrible noises that made me sound like some kind of circus freak, yet which were the only thing that could relieve that terrible, aching pressure that seemed to grow and engulf me when I tried to ignore it. Meanwhile, the other kids were trying to finish the worksheets I had already handed in long ago, and they could always hear me in the background, a continual grunting, tapping annoyance. It wasn't long before they started to lash out.

It was pretty horrible. I can't say I blame them: I was over-active and impulsive; I sounded like a horrible parody of a disabled mental patient; I was terrible at sports and had a bad lisp; I was smarter than them and tended to rub it in; overall, I was just weird.

Still, it hurt; they made fun of me constantly, wouldn't let me play with them, and wouldn't let me be alone either. Oh, I always had a few friends, of course, people who I could play with, who would come over to my house and let me forget my worries. But somehow, they were never around when I was in trouble; they knew where the storm was, and stayed away from it. My whole recess was often spent listening to insults and taunts, and all I could do was sit there and take it. Not that the actual insults were that bad; they were, after all, the work of children, crude and stupid, mass-produced, as if I weren't even worth a witty put-down. But I didn't care about that, because I got the idea behind it all; they hated me, all of them, truly and deeply, and enjoyed seeing my pain. It hurt me, made me feel as if there was no point in going on, as if I really were everything they called me, and worse.

Unfortunately, I didn't really have anywhere to turn for help. My teachers, understandably, didn't like me very much—

I was disruptive in class, talked back, and didn't try very hard at my work (although I didn't really need to). At home I had some understanding, but there were still problems. Since we didn't know then that I had Tourette's, everyone thought that my ticking was just me being annoying or disruptive the way I was with everything else. I was constantly being told to stop; I tried to explain that I couldn't, but I wasn't really able to put it into words and nobody believed me. Since I, like most children, trusted my parents' judgment, I started to think that I really was bad to keep doing this when they'd asked me to stop so many times. The same was true of my disruptive behavior in class. The teachers were constantly yelling at me or punishing me. Some tried to be understanding and to talk to me about my behavior, and I appreciated it, but it never helped. It was really terrible, because I truly wished to be good and to please people, but it seemed as if I just kept doing stupid things before I was able to stop and think, and only regretted them afterward. I began to feel overwhelming guilt and shame at my actions, to hate myself for the burden I was to everyone else. Combined with the taunting of the other children, I became more and more depressed. In third grade, I became suicidal.

Perhaps I should explain. By this time, I had already begun the process of distancing myself that would shadow the rest of my life. I retreated into solitude to avoid the pain that almost all my human interactions seemed to bring. At first I would just sit in my room and watch television, constantly, from the moment I got home until I went to sleep. My parents were rightfully worried, and in second grade they began to severely limit my television privileges. Faced suddenly with over-whelming boredom, I at last found my only sanctuary: books.

Many people at this point say that they were transported to far worlds that they could never reach, that Huck Finn and Christopher Robin became their only friends. Not me, though, for I had learned long ago not to make friends, and I knew that I was too out of shape and scared to have ever participated in the grand adventures I read about. Instead, books taught me to observe, to take joy in watching others as they go through life. I came to learn from other people's mistakes, and I became distanced even further from the rest of the world as I tried to become a dispassionate and imperturbable observer.

I had always liked reading, and I was good at it. It started when my mother read to me *A Wrinkle in Time* and the Narnia books, and by first grade she was reading too slow for me and I would sit in her lap, reading ahead as she read out loud, and waiting for her at the end of a page. Eventually, I started taking the books and reading chapters when she wasn't looking, and then reading books entirely on my own. As time passed, reading replaced the role of television, and there was never a time I didn't have a book nearby, with a piece of paper or a little twig to keep my place. I would wait anxiously whenever I had to do something else, trying to rush through conversations and work so I could get back to my book. I read and developed quickly; by third grade I was reading Tolkien and Crichton, and by fifth I felt that there was nothing but Shakespeare and Marx I couldn't handle.

But to get back to my point about suicide: My books opened doors for me on the rest of life, and showed me how happy other people could be. And many of my books contained references to suicide, as many books do. Although the hero would always only toy with the idea, but then reaffirm himself and go on to victory, I began wondering if maybe he hadn't had the right idea in the first place. As I started watching other people and realizing just how pathetic my life was compared to theirs, I became more and more depressed. In third grade, it came to a head: I became miserable all day, and I'd cry myself to sleep every night. I thought about suicide all day, and I never left my room. I didn't try to display my grief and make grand gestures like so many attempted suicides who actually just want to get people's attention; my grief was private, and I suffered silently in my room. I was entirely sure that I'd be better off dead, but I was still scared. I only actually tried to cut myself once, and the pain made me stop almost immediately. I condemned myself for my weakness, and entered a vicious cycle of guilt and depression that lasted for almost a year. In fourth grade, the circle was broken.

At this time in my life, several things happened all at once. First of all, my parents finally decided something was wrong and took me to a neurologist, who immediately diagnosed me and started me on medication. This was perhaps the best single thing ever to happen to me; suddenly I could focus on tasks, remember instructions, and follow rules. And, at long, long last, the ticking was gone from my life. The damage had already been done, though; everyone in the school already hated me and the taunting only got worse when I stopped giving them good reasons.

However, the door that did open up to me was to adults, and especially to my teachers; although I had always been good on tests, they gradually started to like the new me and realized that I was a genuinely intelligent and perceptive person. They started talking to me, encouraging me, and I, for my part, was so touched by this kindness that I started devoting my life to pleasing them, especially the ones that talked to me about my reading and tried to understand people the way I do.

Another change that came after the pills cleared my head and allowed me to think about my life was that I realized I wasn't to blame for the insults and anger I experienced from my peers, and I really saw for the first time how mean they were being. I started hating them instead of myself, and tried to fight back. One day, I shoved one of my tormenters to make him stop, and he fell right over; looking around me, I realized that I was much bigger than most of the others, and I soon found that beating up one of my tormenters could gain me a reprieve of silence for a few days. Although I tried to avoid fighting if I could, it was that day that I realized I was capable of defending myself, and I vowed never to be hurt again.

I finished the process that my books had begun, and cut myself off totally from all human contact. I started watching people, trying to figure out what drove them, as if I were playing with a puzzle. As I realized more and more how stupid and hateful most people were, I started caring less and less about the human race in general. My medications helped me to stay calm, and I took full advantage of it; I stopped myself from ever being excited by pointless things like sports and games, and I faced the taunts and insults with a cold stare. I still kept close contact with my teachers, and I made a few friends, but I always kept those relationships on my terms. I desired total control over my relationships, so that I could never be hurt. I tried to please only teachers who were already pleased by me, who were impressed by the things I was good at. In my relationships with my friends, I always took the dominant position; I always tried to make it clear that I was the smart one, the strong one, the one that led things. Not to say I was mean to my friends; it's just that I wouldn't trust someone unless he had already surrendered totally to me, because I just couldn't make myself take the risk.

It was a lonely time in my life, and it still is; in the last few years, I've found psychology, and begun to really understand people and what drives them, and have learned to sympathize with people I would formerly have written off as stupid jerks. And I've finally begun to find people I can bring myself to trust: my friends, who are as smart as me and know some of what I've gone through, and my teachers, especially my English teachers, whom I'm finally able to talk to as equals and who now help me to expand my view of the world instead of pressing theirs upon me. I've learned to immerse myself in the intellectual community, reading books of philosophy and poetry and questioning them, coming to my own conclusions about the world.

Right now, I think I'm almost at my goal in all this. My

isolation and observation have taught me what isn't important in life, and my reading and my friends have shown me what is. I have a view of the world that really makes sense to me, and I've surrounded myself with people that I love and trust.

But there are times when I still feel that scared little boy inside of me, telling me "Be safe. . . . Be cautious. . . . It's not worth the risk. . . ."

> **Jeremiah Bingham,** 18, Los Alamos, New Mexico

O n a day-to-day basis we are faced with many questions. More often than not, they are simple questions, like whether to go to class or not. Several times throughout my life I have been faced with one particular question, one that is simple, but very difficult to face, much less answer. That simple yet difficult question was, "Am I gay?" The answer to that question is and always will be yes.

While I was going through that daily internal struggle, I maintained a facade. I did not want other people to know that I was struggling with my sexuality. The realization of my sexuality was gradual. After I had come to terms with myself, I gradually let selected people know about my homosexuality. I had made the decision not to tell my parents until after I was out of high school.

After I had come to terms with my sexuality, I began to feel tired of hiding. Eventually my parents inquired about my sexuality. Unprepared for this, I told my parents that I did not know, buying myself time. During that time a wonderful friend of mine gave me advice about how to talk to my parents. When my time was up, the truth was out and so was I. My parents do not accept my "choice" to be a homosexual, but gradually we are making progress in rebuilding the relationship between us.

Hopefully, as time passes, my family and I can reach a balance. Hopefully they will look at me as their son and see past the labels society has placed on me.

Now a question is facing you: when you see me will you see me as a student, or will you see me as a homosexual student? When I look at people, I do not see religion, race, orientation, gender, or any other label. I am faced with the question, "Whom do you see," and I see people, but that is my answer. You may have another.

> **Matt Tupps,** 14, Bucyrus, Ohio

When I entered Bucyrus High School, I became a part of the cycle of the "first impression" phenomenon. The visual appearance of the student body is the one aspect that had the greatest impact upon me the first few days. I have spent the last nine years in a rural, country school. Most of the students were dressed in a fairly simple manner, with no radical statements made through their physical appearance. I never saw a lip or tongue piercing. Only on Halloween did hair have an unusual color. Jet black hair was not normal. It seems to me that some students feel that the only way to get attention or a reaction from their peers is to make this so-called fashion statement. I find this difficult to understand. Maybe some of the students think that I look like a country hick. I guess that I will just have to do a great deal of watching and will reserve my opinion till later. First impressions are just that, first thoughts, and not lasting beliefs.

▷Brad Oberlander, 15, Bucyrus, Ohio

I t was worse than I had thought. I wasn't even in the building for more than two minutes when I heard it first. "Man, he's short." It came as no surprise to me though. I just couldn't help but wonder how people could be so thoughtless. Then I heard someone else say, "I wonder what he's doing down there?" From my right I heard, "Hey, kid, try growing!" and from my left I heard, "What are you, twelve?" Within my first five minutes of high school, I had been made fun of and put down at least half of a dozen times; and it hit me. It was then that I knew that it was going to be a long school year. While laughter echoed through my ears, I had begun my long journey.

▷Ryan Kelley, 18, Ekron, Kentucky

A NOTE AND A SCAR

J acob always walked slow. Now that I think of it, a turtle could have beaten him to class if we had ever attempted a race. Maybe it was his head, so overloaded with the thoughts he held deep inside. He hadn't a soul to share them with and neither I nor anyone else could have given a care as to what he thought. When we looked at Jake our eyes caught only what they wanted to: the oversized ears on the undersized head, the out-of-style hair that matched his out-of-style clothes, and the scar just above his right eye, in between the eye itself and the brow. That ounce of a scar could only be seen if you got close enough to look into his eyes. It was invisible to the world unless you stared long into his black pupils that seemed to sink all the way into the furthest corner of his head. This scar (along with the other traits I mentioned) branded Jake as one of the easiest targets for the entire school to make fun of.

I'd like to take a minute to concentrate on the significance of the scar, simply because it was quite out of place. While his face was misshapen it was still clean, not a blemish on it. Nonetheless he was still made fun of . . . frequently.

When he first came he hadn't a friend in the world. For obvious reasons, Jake was different. We knew he was, and he knew he was. I could read it in his eyes, the way he walked, and in the scar. It was more than all those, though. It was something that he knew deep inside that none of us did. Yes, Jake was definitely different, and at our school different was nothing to be proud of.

The beginning of his day was always the same; I watched him from my position on the steps in front of the school. He began his mornings with a dose of Eric Jones. Eric would do his little routine like a job, like someone was paying him (I wouldn't have been surprised) to pick on Jake. Through all the name calling and ear pulling, amid every charley horse and backpack dump-out, Jake kept a straight face. He held his own by walking slow, holding his head high, and keeping his lips melted together. Eric's choice number to pull on Jake was making fun of the scar. Simply because the first time he tried, Jake's eyes watered up. He didn't cry. Not a tear was shed. Perhaps if one had been Eric would have been satisfied and left Jake alone. But the tear was a trophy that Jake wasn't willing to give to Eric. Jake never cried, never.

After a full serving of Eric the real tormenting started with my crowd. Names that I prefer to keep to myself for obvious reasons were tossed at Jake like rice at a wedding. He took it, though, and didn't say a word. Maybe it was this that made him so odd, his silent stands against those who humiliated him. Everyone else always ran away or cried. Jake's reactions, however odd they might have been, only fueled our desire to hurt him, make him feel less human.

The rest of Jake's day was quite similar, he was in a constant state of torment. Still none of it seemed to have an effect on him, and the only time I ever saw his lips open or heard any sounds escape from his vocal cords were when Mrs. Greene called on him to answer questions in biology.

That Monday was different, though. I knew when I woke up that morning. It was a feeling deep inside that something was going to happen, but I had no idea what. It was such a scary feeling that I debated whether or not even to get out of bed. Yet I did, and I walked to school and waited for the ball to drop, hoping I was just being superstitious.

That day seemed to go normally until lunchtime. I watched a gang aim their sights at Lou, a boy much like Jake, only when he was teased he awarded his tormentors with tears and sobs. They started with mixing his milk and turkey sandwich together. One of my friends (I feel embarrassed to call him that now) grabbed Lou's face and shoved it into the concoction that had been created on the lunch tray. This had never been attempted before. Teasing and poking, yes, but never any true physical contact (other than a few charley horses). That's when it happened. Out of the corner of my eye I saw Jake rise from his seat. Eyes burning like fire, he stood up and walked like David to Goliath. I watched him in awe with the rest of the lunchroom as he burst his way through the crowd and grabbed my friend's shirt collar. Jake fixed his blazing red eyes on those of my friend and said, in a voice I couldn't recognize, "STOP!" In all my life I had never seen anything like the look my friend had, the stupefied face as readable as the whiteness on it. Jake let go of the shirt collar and my friend took off out of the school. As I watched the fire burn out of Jake's eyes and turn back into the black ash pupils, he bent over and whispered something into Lou's ear, and then returned slowly back to his seat.

Something had struck me as odd during the whole of the "occurrence." I debate whether to tell you this, seeing that it might cause some to doubt the rest of my testimony, but I assure you, I only tell the truth. While Jake's manner was that of utter rage, something just above his right eye seemed to glow. I hesitate in saying this but it was almost as if his scar were shining. It was a faint glimmer so it could have been the light reflecting, but light doesn't usually reflect off the eye, it reflects itself off the forehead. This faint glimmer stayed on his face until he seemed to calm down and sit back at his table. I swear to you that is the truth and I will not say any more about it.

I now watched him through different eyes. I focused on him, trying to figure out why, or better yet how he did what he did. I carefully fixed my eyes on him while he finished his lunch. I watched him as he sat up to take his tray to the lunch lady. He seemed like the same Jake, like nothing at all had just happened.

I turned back to my lunch, happy the deed was done, and that it had nothing to do with me. While stunned, I thought myself free and rested easy. Then I heard the crash. I turned slowly to see Danny Robertson with food all over his letter jacket and Jake standing with a now clean tray because whatever had been on it was now on Danny. Jake stood there with his eyes fixed on the brute as if he were trying to stare right through him, maybe with the false hopes that Danny was doing the same to him. I could tell, however, that Danny was looking into Jake, at the red face, the scar and all. He took hold of Jake by the shirt and ordered him to meet him after school at the parking lot. Jake didn't acknowledge that he had heard the words, but Danny didn't wait for a response. He simply dropped Jake and stormed off through the cafeteria doors.

Jake had dead man written all over him. I knew that if he actually showed at the parking lot, there was a mighty good chance he wouldn't walk home. Danny was the captain of the football team and participated in almost every other sport that he could earn a scholarship for. He got the girls, the cars, and anything he wanted, and now he was going to get Jake's head on a plate.

I followed Jake to fourth and sat out of my seating order right behind him. I couldn't take my eyes off him. I watched him all through the period and he didn't look scared in the least. He simply took notes and paid attention to everything Mrs. Greene had to say. Then at 2:50 he took out a sheet of paper and began to write furiously, too fast to be taking notes. Some driving force was taking hold of him, making his pen fly across the piece of paper. I wanted to see what he was writing, but I was too afraid to ask. Instead I tried to stick my head over his shoulder but I only got the tip of the desk in my view.

The bell rang at 3:00 and everyone ran out to the parking lot. Jake got up last, strapped his backpack on, and walked to the doors. He turned back to me and I noticed his watery eyes. I sat up straight, packed all my stuff together, and raced through the doors following close behind Jake. I stayed behind him as he walked out of the doors into the torture that awaited him.

The crowd formed a sort of corridor, and I could see Danny waiting on the end. Jake walked this hall of shame, living a nightmare of demons and witches who tore and devoured him with their words and spells of humiliation. He walked past them, giving them a tear, one tear. When Jake reached the end of the corridor, Danny paused. He must have been surprised to see that tear roll down the cheek to the tip of Jake's chin. Jake brought his hands from his sides to the air and held them palms facing upward as if asking, "Why, why is it like this?" Danny reared back and let his fist fly. He landed it dead in Jake's right eye, sending him flying back to the ground. He hit the scar that Eric made fun of so much, the scar that seemed to shine when he told everyone to back off Lou, this same scar was now spurting blood out like a faucet. I watched along with everyone as the limp mass fell to the ground, staining the blacktop red. As he made his descent to the earth a note dropped out of his backpack. Danny didn't waste a second. He pounced on Jake like a lion on its prey. I jumped for the note, saving it from the blood that seemed to stream from Jake's face. Someone pulled Danny off of the beaten body, but I wasn't paying attention to who. I was simply looking into the eyes of the boy that I knew had just met his end while opening the note that had found its way into my hands . . . it read . . .

> *There is a time or a place*
> *an area of space that was meant for my self,*
> *this time this place*
> *this area of space I'll never see nor know*
> *The illuminating truths that glare as the sun*
> *will never be seen by the blind ones*
> *and the fear they feel will never end*
> *and there will never be time to understand*

I knew then that the tear he cried wasn't caused by the tormentors. Oh, no, I knew it was quite the opposite. It was shed for them. Amid all the destroyed feelings, all the whippings of words a tear was shed for them. A tear with a prayer, a prayer without a prayer, for it prayed for the reversal of the demons into valiant knights, and the witches into princesses and the spells of humiliation into songs of joy and happiness. That tear that stained the blacktop wet right before he stained it red. That tear burned like fire and it held within a hope for a new beginning for his enemies.

The administrators came, the police and ambulance came, and the parents came, but all were too late. Jake lay there and I knelt beside him with the note in my hand and an understanding in my head that he was right. Jacob, the boy that everyone picked on and saw for an idiot, was the only one who knew the truth about us, and we hated him for it, but above all we feared him for it.

I seized Jacob by his bloodstained T-shirt, shaking him, screaming to him that I understood. But he was gone and I could do nothing now. He was gone, leaving the world with only a note and a scar to be remembered by.

Part III

Our Selves

10

Playing to Win

TO GUARANTEE POPULARITY in the average American high school, a guy must be able to claim either one of two assets: good looks or athletic prowess. Taken separately, only success in athletics can secure total acceptance, since physical appearance scores points only with the female constituency of the student body. Being a star athlete in high school is the quickest, most surefire way to ensure respect and admiration from all students. I came to this scientific conclusion the summer before my freshman year.

I had always loved playing soccer. I joined the team every year throughout elementary and junior high school. But all this time my ability level, relative to other players, was average at best. Even though I would have my occasional good stretch of game performances, my reputation among my classmates never changed. I eventually became complacent and accepted my role as an average player, losing almost all motivation to get better because it just seemed too difficult an endeavor. Whatever your reputation, changing it is never easy. Once you're labeled a stoner, a nerd, or a mediocre player, it takes nothing less than a miracle to alter the popular opinion. But that's exactly what I did after attending a soccer camp the summer before I entered high school.

I was the only person from my junior high team at this particular camp. No one had ever seen me play before. It felt like I was given a second chance to build a name for myself on the soccer field, even if it would only last for one summer. Little did I know how far-reaching the consequences of that summer's events would be.

It just so happened that I had one of my good stretches of play performance the first week I arrived at the camp. Shortly thereafter, I was awarded a starting position on one of the camp's six teams. This did wonders for my confidence at the time, but I wondered how long I could keep fooling the coaches about my ability; surely it would not take long for me to revert back to my old "average" self. However, the fear of being discovered as a fraud was just the motivation I needed.

I practiced all day, paying close attention to the coaches' advice and working harder than ever to improve my skills. After weeks of trying to keep my ruse going I started to realize that my cover as a star soccer player would not be blown for one simple reason: I could not go back to my old self because my old self no longer existed. I had revolutionized my game and along with it my self-confidence. I had become the very star soccer player that I had been pretending to be.

I returned to school the following fall with a mission, to join the varsity soccer team as a freshman and dispel any and all notions of myself as only an average player.

As it turned out, I made the team as well as a great impression on the people at school. I began to notice the positive consequences of my much improved talents on the soccer field immediately. People started to treat me differently. I was given a lot more attention and respect. In short, I was getting a lot more popular.

The better I played on the field, the more liked, respected, and appreciated I was by my peers. This phenomenon was most pronounced on game days, when players were required to wear their jerseys to school. Girls smiled more, teachers called on me first, and people I didn't even know wished me luck on the game. The jersey was my biggest trophy ever. It was like a shield, protecting me against ridicule, embarrassing moments, and exclusion. Whenever I had it on, I felt as if nothing could bring me down.

At first, I had a strong urge to wear my jersey all the time, it had become like a security blanket to me. But gradually, I began to see that the attention I received was not important. It had nothing to do with how I felt, what kind of person I was, or how well I did in school. Sports gave me the confidence I needed. The jersey, however, only stunted my growth and gave me a false sense of self-importance. Whenever I think about high school sports, I think about the games, the guys, the sweet taste of victory and the pure joy of scoring my first goal. Meanwhile, the jersey is all but forgotten. If I remember correctly, it's collecting dust somewhere in my parents' attic.

When I started compiling letters for this book, sports was one of the issues uppermost on my mind. While my experiences with soccer had turned out overwhelmingly positive, I'd always known that it might have easily gone another way. I can only imagine the frustration that Charlie Stein describes in his story, "A Quarterback's Perspective from the Field, Not the Sidelines," as he watches the starting quarterback dropping the ball time and again, while his own, already proven, abilities lie unrecognized by his coach. Had I not gone to soccer camp when I did, I could very well have wound up in Charlie's shoes.

Jason Crayne's story of drug use on the football team also hits home. Although I don't know what I would have done in his place, Jason's attempt to strike a blow against drugs is courageous to say the least. When he first joined the team, he realized that getting stoned and drinking was what his school's football players did best. But it didn't bother him so much until he fell in love with the game and with winning. At odds with his teammates, Jason describes how his football-playing days turned into one never-ending nightmare.

Some might wonder why anyone in their right mind would put up with so much trouble and opposition for a game. To those people, I say read "Blink of an Eye," by Phillip Dawkins. Phillip's loving depiction of the game and its many intricacies borders on the rhapsodic. In his mind, as in the mind of any serious athlete, the game is elevated to an art form. There's so much joy to be found within the confines of the court that a basket is less the sum of its points than it is a masterpiece.

The excitement of watching a game is what Adam Levine describes in his "Those Summer Nights." Anyone who doesn't understand why guys love sports with such a passion needs only to read this essay. The ritual of choosing a team and rooting for it is passed down from father to son for generations. It's a pleasure that few men can ever outgrow; in fact, unlike the childhood craving for sugar and the adolescent affinity for loud music, our love for sports only increases with the years.

The next two entries both deal with cross-country running. While the first is a poem by Atif Zohair Qadir and the second a narrative by Kevin DeAnna, the two pieces might as well have been written by the same person, so similar are the sentiments expressed in their respective works. Next to running, everyday life is nothing more than a game of Trivial Pursuit, far removed from the physical demands of our existence. As the ultimate primal act, running brings both Atif and Kevin in touch with their primitive natures.

Finally, Salvatore Leo's essay about an old, dilapidated stadium from his youth really captures what sports mean to today's boys. More than just a way to stay in shape, score with girls, and learn discipline, sports becomes the activity through which boys find their place in the world and build upon it. Even more important, sports is the connection that binds us together, giving us a common purpose and a reason to win.

> **Charlie Stein,** 16, Great Neck, New York

A QUARTERBACK'S PERSPECTIVE
FROM THE FIELD, NOT THE SIDELINES

Since seventh grade, I have been a member of the Rebels football teams. Each year my playing time has varied greatly. In seventh grade, I saw no action except the action on the sidelines. Let me say it wasn't a very eventful year! Eighth grade was a breakthrough year. I went out as a quarterback, and ended up starting as "B" team QB. Our team went 5–1. Ninth grade was, however, another season of total boredom from the sidelines. This year, I returned with hopes of actually starting a game. In the first game, I played, but only at the end as we were getting blown away. That day, I heard that I would be starting our next game, our home opener.

The instant I heard the news, I went to Dan Shanks, our starting QB, and asked him why he wasn't going to be at the game. He spoke words that were joy and utter delight to my ears: "I have to go to California for my aunt's wedding."

To say that I was excited would be an understatement. I felt that this was my chance to break through, show what I had, and maybe even earn a starting role. The next week of practice I made sure I perfected everything. By Thursday, my throwing, pitches, handoffs and footwork were perfect. Nothing was going to obstruct my path to victory.

Friday night: constant dreams about the game. Accomplishing everything, doing everything right. The clearest vision: the touchdown pass that won the game.

Saturday morning: Arrived at locker room, dressed, mentally prepared for the festivities ahead. Received new football from Coach Calhoun, examined it for imperfections, tucked it under my arm. No one was touching that ball. Victory was written all over it.

First quarter: So used to flipping out and not going onto the field, forgot to go in! Gave tiny inspirational speech to huddle: "Yo, listen up. Let's go out and run all over them! It's our first official game, and we are NOT going to be beaten on our home turf!" Rough first set—moved ball a mere six yards. Still confident.

Second quarter: Threw touchdown pass. Small celebration in end zone followed by a failed play. Home 6, Visitors 0.

Third quarter: Not much action. My thirty-yard pass intercepted.

Fourth quarter: Threw the game-winning pass. Smile from Calhoun, cheers from crowd. Home 20, Visitors 19.

We had won! I took off my helmet and raised it into the air. I was pumped, I didn't want to stop playing. After shaking hands with our opponents, we held a final team meeting, where I was congratulated and cheered. It was amazing how much respect I received for the next couple of days. This was definitely the most exciting and incredible event of this year.

I had played pretty well that day and thought that I would have a legitimate chance to start the next game. Practice the next week proved me wrong. Dan came and took his spot back. Benched again.

This is how it remains today. Calhoun hasn't bothered to put me back at the helm once since that game. At the end of every game that Dan doesn't play his best, I'm filled with anger. I have sat so often it's aggravating. I watch us fall apart. I feel that I am good enough to make a difference, even if only as a receiver.

But old traditions have come back. I only go into the game if we are up or down by a lot. Calhoun hasn't put me in since our solitary victory. I burn inside because I want to go in so badly, but I don't know what to say to him. We'll see what happens the rest of this year—there's still the chance that Dan will have to go back to California.

⟩Jason Crayne, 17, New City, New York

When I first started playing football, I thought it was a great idea. It would be lots of fun. People would admire me because I was on the football team. Maybe I would get more girls. I could strut around school in my jersey and feel cool. That was the original idea. It got a lot more complicated than that, though.

I found out real fast that at my school, sports and drugs went hand in hand. You couldn't play a football game unless you'd had eight beers and a few joints the night before. Hell, after the game you had sixteen beers and seven or eight smokes. It bothered me a lot. It didn't bother me that there were guys doing this. I couldn't care less what they did to themselves. What bothered me is that there were guys on this football team who worked their asses off, day in and day out, and put everything they had into this football team. And come game day, my team went down in flames because these guys had to go out drinking and smoking the night before.

They didn't care about the team. I don't know if they even cared about winning. I know they didn't care about their fellow teammates, who wanted nothing more than to play football and win. Things got worse, though. It got to the point where the team was actually divided—guys who were clean and wanted to win, and guys who smoked/drank and just wanted to f—around. Imagine that—a football team, supposed to be a tight brotherhood, its members ready to defend each other, was about to come to blows over whether or not we wanted to win. It was absurd—yet it was there.

A lot of these guys were angry and frustrated that we were losing. I suggested at one point that maybe we were losing because they were boozing the night before. Because of that suggestion, I made a lot of enemies on the team. My closest friend, a captain, became the scapegoat for all the resentment, spite, and frustration from these druggies. They were angry we couldn't win, and they blamed him. They were also angry that he spoke to the coaches about the drug problem on our team. They struck back at my friend—curses, insults in the hallway. They keyed his car, they smeared dog droppings on his locker. All this because a guy wanted to win? Because he wanted a clean team, was ready to play football and not roll over and quit?

Sports aren't all they are made out to be. They aren't the clean, pure competition that they originally were. What they are is a daily struggle, often against your teammates in addition to the opposing team. It hurts that the exhilaration of winning has been abandoned for the highs of weed and the drunken stupor of a Budweiser. But it isn't going to change unless we, regardless of whether we are athletes or not, decide that we aren't going to stand for it anymore. Nothing will ever change until we decide to do something about it.

▶ **Phillip Dawkins,** 14, Elk Grove, California

BLINK OF AN EYE

Offense, Defense.
Two worlds completely different
Yet exactly the same.
Existing together in perfect harmony on the court,
Unable to exist without each other.
Able to fire a three one minute,
And get a steal the next.
Viewed as a threat by either side.
Looked at by the defense as
The stopper, the ender of control.
Always the opposition.

With a quick stroke,
The ball passes through the net.
With a quick slap,
The ball is batted out of bounds.
Flowing through plays,
Shifting the zone.
Always ready to jump from one world to the next.
It is inevitable that I am in both my worlds,
But not possible to be in both of them at one time.
Always changing at the blink of an eye.

> **Adam Levine,** 17, New City, New York

THOSE SUMMER NIGHTS

When I was a young child, July always was the month that I looked forward to the most. On occasional summer nights, my grandfather would come into my bedroom with an enormous grin on his face, holding a gift that I remember vividly to this day. In his hand lay the excitement that was overwhelming for any young child, tickets to the Friday night Mets game.

Naturally the first sport I learned to play as a young American boy was baseball. Everyone in my family, ranging from my father to my grandmother, played baseball with me. On the weekends, my grandmother would take me to the front lawn, and have a catch with me for hours. I always imagined that I was Keith Hernandez, or Gary Carter (my two favorite Mets at the time), as I would roll on my front lawn attempting to catch balls that she threw to me. I would even wear my hat backward like Gary Carter, or attempt to get my clothes dirty, in an attempt to emulate Keith Hernandez's dirt-stained uniform.

I always looked forward to seeing my grandfather enter my

bedroom with tickets that opened a magical world of excitement for me. On the following Friday night, my grandfather, father, and I would pack our bags with sandwiches, potato chips, soda, my baseball glove, sweatshirts, and a bunch of napkins for the car. Besides baseball, my other real passion was spilling my food all over myself and everyone sitting around me. As we would head south on the Palisades Parkway toward the Big Apple, my father would tell me to take a nap so that I could stay up late and watch the entire game. As any five-year-old would do, I argued with him about not wanting to, and then fell asleep in the backseat within a few short minutes.

On most occasions, I would get up right before we entered the stadium parking lot. The sound of what I thought were other happy New York Mets fans honking their horns as a celebration, as they entered the stadium would be my pre–Mets game alarm clock. Later, I realized that these "happy fans" were not as happy as all that. Rather, they were the typical New York drivers in a rush to get a parking spot close to the stadium entrance.

When we entered Shea Stadium, my little jaw would drop open in awe. The bright green lawn shone radiantly with the massive "Royal Crown Cola, Welcome to Shea Stadium" scoreboard in the distance. Back in those years, the players would come out early, and sign autographs for some lucky fans. Those who read this may think that I am a senior citizen, because players don't always do this anymore. We never sat close enough to get an autograph, but I loved to watch the ball dugout entrance, hoping to see one of my two favorites pop out.

As the game started, my grandfather and I would always talk about how we would love to catch a foul ball. Being such a young child, I never realized that I would have such a slim chance of catching one, but I always watched the game intensely, hoping for the chance.

My father and grandfather still laugh about how I once slept through half of a game. I was so sound asleep when we arrived at the stadium that my father decided to carry me still sleeping into the stadium. He assumed that the sound of the fans cheering would wake me up. However, that was not the case. Apparently, I had been so excited about the tickets all week, it had tired me out. I did not wake up until the fifth inning. I turned around and saw my grandfather and dad laughing, since they couldn't believe that I could miss that much of the game that I had looked forward to all week. Although I was really upset that I missed half of my beloved Mets game, I cheered up quickly, and rooted for my team as they continued to win the game.

To this day, I go to the baseball games with my grandfather and father. Now, my younger brother joins us too. We still pack the car with sandwiches, potato chips, soda, my baseball glove, sweatshirts, and a bunch of napkins, (some things never change), and start our all-American all-guys night.

> **Atif Zohair Qadir,** 17, East Patchogue, New York

A RUNNING SONNET

The glowing afternoon warmth weighs on me.
The burnt asphalt below, each rise and fall
Makes earth standing waves that beckon and call.
An escape from urban life watched closely.
I run, float, stride and glide; finally free
Like *Homo sapi'ns* of old: hunt and all.
Days "uncivilized": life that may appall.
Tear the ties that make each man's blood weary!

Few follow instinct. Life is soci'ty.
But I can hear my breath and feel muscle.
In this, I've found a way to simpler days.
Unbounded by time, money, propri'ty.

I feel glory, pain and strength; not hustle.
Man's sinew-woven: a natural maze.

> **Kevin J. DeAnna,** 16, Cedar Grove, New Jersey

REFLECTIONS OF A RUNNER

It was a cold morning in late fall as over one hundred teenagers lined up across a grass field in central New Jersey.
Some shivered as the bitter wind cut into their exposed legs
and arms as surely as a knife of steel. A few leaped up and
down in last-minute agitation. The more philosophical spit con-
templatively onto the ground while others, with intense looks
suitable to marching to war, cleansed their nostrils by applying
pressure to one side, blowing violently, and then repeating the
process on the opposite side. At this moment, and in this place,
it seemed as though the entire world was focused on the events
taking place in Holmdel, New Jersey.

The teens, the best boys from the Group 1 classification of
New Jersey high schools, gazed out at the hilly terrain before
them. Their eyes narrowed. They had come from all over the
state, and the resulting collision of skin and uniform colors gave
the impression of a huge multicolored python slithering across
the grass. Friends and complete strangers whispered anxiously
among themselves as time slowly, agonizingly, and yet unremit-
tingly, ticked away. Mixed among the general silence were scattered cries of anxiousness or even outright fear, disguised as yells
of encouragement. Coaches and parents said some last words to
the boys and then were moved beyond a set boundary, thus
abandoning their protégés to whatever lay ahead.

An older man, dressed in a blood red jacket and gaudy
yellow shirt, strode confidently to the front of the crowd. His

eyes were hard and businesslike and he gave off the manner of a Marine drill sergeant. He barked out a series of commands and instructions to the youths that were assembled. These were mostly ignored, as the boys had heard similar exhortations countless times before. It was the bitter end of the season; even the freshmen that were present were grizzled veterans. The man reached for a pistol and, grasping it, raised it into the air. Some of the boys regarded the weapon as though the man were going to shoot them with it. Others welcomed the sight, because it showed that they were about to take part in something that was the culmination, the final result, of hours upon hours of pain, struggle, and sacrifice. All of the boys felt their muscles tighten. There was dead silence. The earth stood still.

Suddenly, the quiet was shattered by the sharp crack of the gun. The tranquil scene became a maelstrom of absolute chaos as the boys stumbled over one another and rushed forward. It was a giant stampede of wild-eyed and somewhat panicked adolescents. The giant buffalo herds of the American West had returned and were charging across of the grasslands of New Jersey. Inside the herd, there was no time for thought as all effort was concentrated on maintaining one's place amid a sea of feet, arms, and elbows. Above the din of the grunts and the sounds of heavy breathing, one could hear several of the runners talking to each other, anxious to get in one last word before their lungs would be stripped of oxygen. Suddenly, a rhythmical chant could be heard emitting from the swarming mass. It started with one team and it spread to the others. Even those runners at the front of the pack could be seen smiling, although they were not taking part. The chant became so loud that it overwhelmed the grunts, overwhelmed the yells, and overwhelmed the sounds of lungs gasping for air.

"Running—SUCKS!" "Running—SUCKS!" "Running—SUCKS!"

What is it about the sport of cross-country that makes people devote their entire high school sports career to it? It is mocked probably more than any other sport. If someone asks what sport you play, the response to an answer of "cross-country" is a contemptuous snort, and a cry of "Oh, that's not even a real sport." Other common retorts include: "How can you just *run*?" "Are you crazy?" "What is the matter with you?" "*Why?*" You see, in every other sport, running is considered a punishment, such as "Johnson, run five laps because you were talking." However, in cross-country, running *is* the sport. What every other kind of athlete considers synonymous with pain and misery, a cross-country runner considers his job, his sport, and to a certain degree, his life. Almost no one actually *enjoys* the pain of running, and thus serious runners adopt a fatalistic attitude toward their sport that carries over into their perspective toward the events of everyday existence. For others, sports are a way to have fun. For runners, cross-country is a job, a serious job, and one that is not to be trifled with.

It is such a simplistic sport and yet it is without question the hardest, and, externally, the least rewarding sport. There are no cheerleaders and no pep band. There is very little newspaper coverage. Certainly no one comes to the meets except for a parent or two. Most students do not even know the sport exists. No trophies, no triumphant team parties after the game (most runners are too tired even to talk after the race). It is a sport that inflicts excruciating pain as a matter of course. What makes any sane person pick this sport?

I don't know. As a cross-country runner of three years now, I still don't know what I was thinking. Perhaps it was as simple as the fact my father had done it and it didn't *seem* all that bad. Now I look back and wonder if I was drunk when I signed. There is something even more amazing about this. I would not be able to stop now, even if I tried. I hate the pain—every morning I curse myself for picking this sport before going out to run—and yet day after day, week after week, I continue to train.

I have become addicted to the feeling one gets after a hard

run. The entire day I feel indolent and lazy, sick even, until I have run. On the day of a race, the upcoming athletic event dominates the entire day. It is as though I can't even hear what other people are saying. Teachers and my fellow students talk to me, asking me to listen to them, and I just nod with a blank stare, thinking all the while, "What is the matter with you people? Don't you know I have a race today?" And I know I am not alone. I have talked to runners on other teams and the serious ones all feel the same way. I have heard stories of runners coming to school sick just so they can make it to the meet for the privilege of putting their already weakened body in excruciating pain for about twenty minutes. I hear stories of people running extra workouts or forsaking jobs or another sport just so they can hurt their body a little bit more.

Runners display a singular comradeship with one another, an idiosyncrasy unique to the sport. One hears of football teams trash talking or basketball teams fighting after the game. Runners don't fight with each other. Perhaps it is simply because they are too out of breath to trash talk or too tired after a race to fight but I think it is something more. Everyone who has run will read this and understand what I am saying. Every cross-country athlete on the planet shares a bond with every runner that cannot be broken. We all know what it is like and we are going through the same thing. Thus, runners feel more like companions on some important quest than bitter enemies fighting to destroy each other. Even rival runners who have trained for months just to defeat their antagonist will greet each other before the race and wish each other luck. Rarely will such an occurrence happen between football rivals. Besides, runners know that we do not compete against one another. We compete against ourselves.

We compete against our cowardice, our willingness to surrender or quit, our sloth, our laziness every time we lace up our shoes. We feel it when we are out for a long-distance run and we can feel the fatigue building in our thighs. We feel it during an interval workout when we feel that our lungs will explode with one more breath. We feel it during a race when we could swear that we will pass out at any moment—believe me, we would welcome it. However, for some reason, we keep going.

The scene I described before was from the Group championships for cross-country in New Jersey. It takes place in Holmdel, New Jersey. It is a course held in reverence and fear by current and former runners all over the state. It contains some of the toughest hills one will find on any course, hills that devastate even the most determined runner. The following week, the all-Group championships, with the best runners in the state, is held. The last time this event took place, the winner of the Group 1 race was running in the top five. His blood sugar became depleted and he ran into a tree. He also passed out twice. After the race, he was taken to a hospital. The most incredible part of the story was that he was able to finish.

What is it about this sport that asks for—and receives—such sacrifice? For the vast majority of runners, a few medals, a word of congratulations from a coach, maybe someday a one-line mention in the local paper is all one can ask for. Yet, people keep running. All of us—we keep on going. There is some driving force within us that keeps us moving. There may be no glory, no parties, or huge school pep rallies for the cross-country team but there is *something*, some internal satisfaction that cannot be matched by anything else.

We live in a superficial world, and believe me, a high school is the ultimate in superficiality. It is a world of endless home-work assignments, petty feuds, a myriad of problems that arise each day and will be solved and forgotten before lunch. As important as school is, there is a feeling of cheapness, or, better, unreality to it. It is like we are divorced from the real world. For runners, cross-country, as painful and as futile as it may seem to some, is their connection with reality. For me, it is the

most important thing that I will do each day. I will never feel
more alive than I do at the end of a race. I will never feel more
proud or satisfied with the person of Kevin J. DeAnna than I
will at the end of a 3.1-mile challenge that others cannot even
begin to comprehend. Each runner takes something different
from the sport, and what I take is a feeling of being alive, in a
way more real and profound than anything else I experience
during the day.

I was among those runners in that race a while back. I was
one of the runners who was chanting against my sport. I hate
the pain. I hate the sacrifice. I hate waking up knowing what
I have to do on the day of a race. But I will not stop, I will not
quit, and I cannot *live*, in the true sense of that word, without
running. Those other runners that were chanting; believe me,
they'll be back.

And so will I.

> **Salvatore A. Leo,** 16, Johnstown, New York

NIPPLE STADIUM

On days when I was younger, instead of sitting around doing nothing, my friends and I created our own tiny world
inside of the town we lived in. We would stay there for hours,
playing a simple game that kept us entertained day and night.
This place was all we had, and all we wanted. One summer day,
we were looking into the sky past home plate, at the brown
tips of the triangular building that sat beyond the field on the
horizon. At that moment we realized we had a name for our
hangout, Nipple Stadium.

Our diamond wasn't a field at all and hardly a stadium.
What we called our stadium was actually a dirty old parking lot
for the sanitation department next to my friend's house. There

was barely any grass. Most of what we played on was pavement.
We have all had our share of cuts and scrapes there, which we
called strawberries. The lot was filled with gravel and pebbles,
with sprouts of grass shooting through in a few spots. The dangerous pavement made the lot an accident waiting to happen.
Right field was a giant wall of tall pine trees that made hitting
a home run in that direction almost impossible. Left and center field were made up of the road outside the parking lot. In
center field there was a tall tree that stood alone, another obstacle to home runs.

The home run boundary used to be the road, but due to
our growth spurts, we eventually extended it another twenty
feet. We used a two-out system to speed up game play. Our old
gloves served as bases, and instead of baseballs and baseball
bats, we played with tennis balls and Wiffle bats.

Everyone had his own bat. We would modify the bats by
putting electrical tape around them so that they would carry
more weight and be more heavy duty. The more weight the
bat carried, the farther the ball would travel. The sides of the
lot were surrounded by a fence with a green cover on it, so
you couldn't see through to the other side. The fence was too
high for us to climb, so when a foul ball went over it, someone
small had to climb under the fence to fetch it. When we went
under, we would get dirty, since we had to scrape against the
ground. Going to fetch the ball was a pain and we argued all
the time about who was to get the ball next.

Oftentimes, the sanitation workers would see us in their
work area and scream at us. One time I was dared to throw
the ball at the guy whose butt always hung out of his pants. So
I crawled under the fence and, with all my friends watching
me through the cracks, I threw the ball at him and then quickly
crawled back under. My friends and I all ran. I'd hit the guy
and he was hollering at us as we ran away. We came back the
next day, though, and kept on playing. The sanitation workers
always threatened to call our parents on us and tell them we

were causing trouble, but they never did. I think they figured we were just a bunch of boys having fun.

Other than that, the neighborhood was a peaceful place. The street led to a dead end, so hardly any traffic went by. The owners of the houses across the street would never get mad when our ball would hit their house or gardens. They would simply ask who was winning the game. And Mr. Jameson would never get angry when he had to get our ball because his dog, Rebel, terrified all of us. The neighborhood seemed like a fictional place. It was never dark, never cloudy, and it never rained. No one ever yelled at us for playing too late or for playing at eight in the morning and waking up the whole street. Nobody. My seven friends and I and the rest of the street became a family in a way. Every day, as we entered that street, we escaped the rest of the town, and the rest of reality. I played with seven of my friends, and we cherished the gift that was given to us. To me, the greatest thing in the world was hanging out with the guys and playing baseball.

One day we decided to have our own world series. It might not sound like much, but for us winning meant having the bragging rights of the summer. We were friends, but for that week, those of us on different teams, we were enemies. We played the best of seven games and we took every game very seriously. Each game was played at noon and lasted about two hours. The series was tied three games to three, and the final game was here.

I was pitching. I had a no hitter going, and at the bottom of the ninth we were winning by one. The pressure was intense. I struck out the last two batters with ease, and I pitched the no hitter. My team won. Winning the world series was the most exciting thing I had ever accomplished. I really felt like it was the world series, and to us it was. My team jumped on me and carried me in the air. We celebrated by rubbing our victory in the other team's face. A couple of the people from the neighborhood even watched.

Then we all got together to decide when the next game was going to be. We played again the next day. Baseball was the best. I loved hanging around and shooting the breeze at nipple stadium just as much as playing. Sometimes we'd just stand there, throwing rocks and joking around for hours. We really loved to hang out together. We were like brothers.

Youth is a precious gift. All of my friends are still around, but we don't hang out like we used to or play baseball. We've all gone our separate ways. Summertime, baseball, hanging with friends, no worries. That's what life was to me. Every day I would get up and have baseball on my mind, that's all. I had no worries. We played baseball every day. But we had no fans, no money, nothing. Just the game. We just loved to play the game. When I reminisce about the days we would play, I cannot remember a rainy day, or a day that the sun wasn't shining. To me, the field is a sacred spot of my youth. Nipple stadium was our paradise, our own heaven. Someday I'm going to go back to the field and see if the bat I threw on the building next to the lot is still there. Or if the hole behind the broken street sign, the one we clogged up with gravel to stop the ball from rolling under the fence, is still there. I will check the parking lot poles to see if they still have marks on them from when we would hit them after striking out. And I will see if there is any electrical tape lying around on the lot. Sometimes I think of playing baseball there again someday, but I realize that will probably never happen. I can still hear the sounds of us playing. The sound of eight young boys playing baseball.

11

Gone Too Soon

I HAVE A SUPERSTITION pertaining to digital clocks. Whenever the time reads 11:11, I try to make as many wishes as possible before the clocks turns to 11:12, hoping they'll come true. Although my wishes vary, depending on the circumstances, my first wish is always the same; good health and longevity for my family, friends, and myself. Out of all the issues young people have to deal with, dealing with the death of a loved one is by far the most difficult. I can't begin to imagine how painful the experience must be. Losing a family member at a young age makes any other problem or obstacle in life seem meaningless and insignificant in comparison.

The letters I received dealing with the death of loved ones all convey a grave sense of bitterness and sadness. Growing up is hard enough without having to be prematurely robbed of the illusions that make our youth so singularly carefree. Those of us who haven't experienced the death of a relative or friend will never truly understand how that one event can inform the rest of our lives and irrevocably change the way we see the world around us.

Tim Dale's very poignant tale "Bed of Roses" is about a

young boy who must come to terms with the car crash that killed his parents. While focusing on the reenactment of the accident, the essay also testifies to the excrutiating emptiness felt by its writer. Once the boy has fully come to grips with what has happened, he visits the burial site of the deceased, and finds out that his soul will not rest until he is reunited with his loving parents.

Gaelan Baillie's "A Loss, but a Gain" tells the story of a his grandmother's death and what he gained when his grandfather moved in after her passing. Although he is extremely saddened by his grandma's death, he finds solace in his grandfather, and vice versa. He realizes that if it hadn't been for her death, he would have never gotten to know his grandfather. By focusing on what he is grateful for rather than the sad thought of his grandma's death, he finds that his faith in life is renewed.

Along these same lines, Joseph Anderson's account of his friend's death sees him honoring his memory not with tears, but with a renewed zeal for life and making every moment count. Although he is extremely saddened by the passing of his courageous young friend, he knows that the best way to honor his memory is to do what his friend would have wanted him to, go on with his life and not take anything for granted.

> **Tim Dale,** 18, Ukiah, California

BED OF ROSES

As Lennox scanned the garden, he couldn't help but admire its darkness. He looked over the bleak, hilly landscape, with its monstrous flowers that seemed to be grinning at him with what looked like teeth. Everything seemed as dark and miserable as those jagged flowers. Even the once beautiful butterflies wore the mark of death upon their crest. All Lennox could do was gaze at their once glorious home. Now only a shell of lost dreams remained. Their once happy lives had been shattered in an instant.

He walked into the lifeless shell, and gazed at the run-down furniture, still covered with now dusty sheets. He picked up a tarnished silver hairbrush and admired its swirling designs. Lennox held the brush to his cheek. Immediately a dark haze draped over his mind; the images of two souls converging, and becoming one in the eyes of family and friends. Lennox opened his eyes and smiled in a moment of sweet remembrance.

He then made his way to the garage. Lennox unmasked terrifying memories, as he gazed upon the red sports car that had been restored, but still bore scars from a tragic night. The images of the same two souls driving down a dark mountain road. In the rear seat was a baby soul, giggling and laughing with innocence, smiling and wiggling with joy. The two souls, holding hands, feeling the happiness emanating from each other's fingertips.

Lennox opened his eyes once again. Tears started to stream down his cheeks. He buried his face in his hands and wept. All he could see when he closed his eyes were two bright lights. He knew the these two bright lights were the bearer of death. Lennox then threw the brush across the room with a wave of grief so intense it blinded him. Lennox stumbled into the car. As soon as he sat down a hellish image attacked his mind. An image of jagged steel, glass, and blood followed by flashing blue and white lights. He saw the small soul lying in the rain a few feet away from its mother, who was engulfed in blood. A few minutes prior, he had felt the energy from this now lifeless soul. Her once white complexion was now tainted red.

Lennox freed himself from the car and fled the shadows of the shell. He found himself back in the garden once again. The landscape looked the same, except two uneven strips of the rose bed were dug up. Lennox walked over to the roses and stood over the strips. He looked down into the dark, cold earth. He saw the two lifeless souls lying peacefully in the ground. Lennox looked at their broken faces and lost all emotional control. As tears poured from his eyes, he thought about the times he could have had with the souls. He mourned over the lost time; time that would have made his life complete, instead of condemned.

Lennox went back to his bench and stared at his garden for the last time, as he wept with sorrow. Then, his otherwise dark heart lit up with one reassuring thought. Lennox couldn't think of a better place for these two pure, peaceful, and loving souls to lie at rest than in a bed of roses. To Lennox, the roses showed how fragile the two souls were. One day Lennox would join them in that rose bed, and only in the cold earth would Lennox's heart become warm again.

> **Gaelan Baillie,** 15, Niagara Falls, New York

A LOSS, BUT A GAIN

I never knew how it felt to be so sad and depressed until my grandma died. She went to the doctor's office for a regular checkup, and never came back.

She went to the doctor on February 14, 1996. It was a rainy Wednesday. When I came home from school that day, someone called from the hospital and said that my grandma had to get surgery; it was serious. She went under anesthesia, and during the surgery, she had a stroke. She never woke up, but she was still alive because of the machines. The doctors turned them off and took out her tubes. I never got to say good-bye.

She died on February 19, 1996, a Monday morning. I had a terrible headache the whole day. All my aunts, uncles, cousins, relatives, and people I had never seen before came over to my house. There must have been at least fifty people hanging around. I didn't stay there that much. I went out and hung around with my friends. It was too hard to see all of my family members crying. Everything in my house reminded me of my grandma.

Seeing pictures of her and old gifts that she gave me was hard to take. Even watching television made me think of her. My grandma and I always used to watch *The Price Is Right* and *Wheel of Fortune* when we got a chance. She would always try to beat me in *Wheel of Fortune*. I used to cry most nights in my room by myself wondering why God took my grandma away. For the rest of that month, I cried myself to sleep.

When I went to her wake there were over two hundred people there to say good-bye and to mourn her death. I hated to see her body lying there in the casket. She was pale and white; almost fake looking. The smell of her favorite fragrance still lingered on her. Her short brown hair was curly, just how she had always worn it. Her facial expression was dull and sad, not like when she was alive. She was always cheerful and happy.

At her funeral my uncle read a eulogy and everyone was crying and sobbing. I never felt so sad. I felt like I'd had the wind knocked out of me. The whole time it seemed to be a dream. I couldn't believe this was happening.

After the funeral, my mom and her brothers asked my grandpa if he wanted to move in and live at my house. He said yes.

It was around the end of February or the beginning of March when my grandpa moved in. At first it was a hard adjustment. I lost my grandma and he lost his wife of forty-seven years. He was so used to the way they lived in their house that it was hard for him to get used to the way I lived in mine. He was never sure what my sister and I were allowed to do. My grandpa would always say, "Wait until your mother gets home and then we'll see what she says" when he didn't know if we were allowed to do something. My grandpa and I used our senses of humor to get along. We talked about when he was a kid, what it was like when he fought in World War II, and many other things. We also talked about my grandma and he told me stories about her and the things she did.

I miss my grandma dearly and I was devastated that she passed away. When my grandpa moved in, it helped me through my grief, and I think it also helped him too. My grandpa moving in was one of the best things that ever happened to me.

▷ **Joseph Anderson,** 17, Tallahassee, Florida

TIME COUNTS

We have all been told, at one point or another, that we should make the most of each and every day. In our modern world of greed, stressful deadlines, and material wants, I think it is hard to see how important each day really is. In fact, I do not think that anyone can fully comprehend this advice until we either arrive in a situation of adversity, have a near death experience, or meet and are influenced by someone who, for one reason or another, knows how important each day can be. I learned this the "easy" way. My friend, Lee, showed me how important it is to make the most of our time.

I met Lee during the early spring of my seventh-grade year. He was on my baseball team; we were Monk's Office Machines of Meridian Park Junior Major League. The first day of practice, Lee walked up to the field with a big, wide grin on his face, ready to play. Lee was different from everyone else on the team. He had fought and survived a battle with cancer when he was younger, but he lost part of his right leg as a result.

Lee was one the best guys anyone could ever want on their

team. He was the epitome of a team player. Although he couldn't run the bases, he still hit and had to run to first before a pinch runner could replace him. Lee played third base for us and rarely made an error. At times, there were balls he couldn't get to, and there were some that he got to but just couldn't make the throw. However, he rarely bobbled the ball. He had to work much harder than anyone else just to be *equal,* yet he did everything with a smile. Lee never complained or used his disability as an excuse.

I truly feel that Lee had a great time playing ball that season. Looking back, I really hope that Lee never thought or felt that he wasn't as big a part of that team as anyone else on the field. If there was ever anything that he was unable to do because of his disability, and I honestly cannot remember if there was, he made up for it in spirit. Lee was always into the game, cheering everyone on. He was always there with an "atta boy" to congratulate his teammates for a good play, or a "you'll get 'em next time" to pick someone up after a bad one. To tell the truth, I and everyone else on that team looked *up* to him, admired him, and were definitely inspired by him. How could anyone not be?

That season, we were nearly unbeaten. Everyone on the team contributed, and each player was the "hero" at one time or another, including Lee. At the end of the season, we ended up league champions, which was a great accomplishment. At the season-ending picnic, we were all announced as the park champs, and we had our chance to run onto the field with our teammates. I can still see the confidence, excitement, and joyful energy in Lee's eyes as he darted across the field. Afterwards pictures were taken, hands shaken, congratulations accepted, and our whole team was just as happy and proud as possible. We felt as if we were on top of the world. Little did we know that all this joy, pride, and excitement would swiftly turn to feelings of grief and loss a mere year later.

I saw Lee a few months later, at a basketball game. He was

getting a drink of water, and I walked up to talk to him. By this time, he no longer had his prosthetic leg, and he was on crutches. The cancer had returned. As we talked, I noticed that he sounded weaker. His voice quivered the slightest amount, but he was still in high spirits. We talked for about five minutes, about school, the basketball game, and even baseball, which only a few months gone, was still fresh in our minds. This would be the last chance I got to talk with Lee.

The call came about four months later, early the next spring. The phone's ring was innocent enough, but the message was one that no one wanted to hear. Lee had died. He had passed away a couple of nights earlier, in his sleep. The cold, grim reality of life struck me, but I didn't fully understand, or believe, until the funeral.

The funeral took place on a chilly, overcast day a week or so later. In the car on the way to the church, it was silent. It wasn't a harsh, unwelcome silence, but a calm, thoughtful silence. Five guys from the team were present, and we all sat together. Before the service began, we talked about, remembered, and even laughed about all the good times we had shared with Lee. We stirred up memories from the previous summer, just one short year earlier. The tears would come later.

Lee was the kind of person that *everyone* loved. He lived his life to the fullest and never let his illness run his life or slow him down. Whatever he did, whether on a field or in any other aspect of his life, he did it with all he had and made the most of every opportunity.

I know that God has a reason for everything, but I don't think his reasons are always within the grasp of human comprehension. Maybe He chose Lee because of his strength, endurance, and ability. Lee had the *ability* to show others that every day counts, that we should make the most of the time we are given.

12

Song of Sorrow

WHEN I THINK of the reasons why I decided to pursue a career in clinical psychology one person always comes to mind, my friend David. We met in elementary school and instantly became friends. David and I were close from the very beginning. We continued to be friends throughout junior and most of senior high school. Our friendship survived my move to a different school district after seventh grade. Spending time with David felt very natural to me, I felt a level of comfort with him that was absent in my other friendships. I considered him my best friend. Aside from me, David didn't have too many friends. But that was OK because we spent most of our time together.

We spoke about every topic under the sun. David always had an opinion on everything, and for the most part our viewpoints complemented each other's. However one issue was always left out of our numerous discussions: David's family life.

I knew he was an only child and that both of his parents worked, but that was about as far as my knowledge went on the issue. At the infrequent times I would ask him a question about his parents, David's responses would invariably be terse and unemotional. However, I never thought anything of it. I figured that as with most teenagers, his relationship with his parents was probably far from perfect.

This all changed the day I decided to pay an unannounced visit to David's house. As I approached his front doorstep I heard what sounded like a loud argument between David and his father. I was about to leave when the front door opened and David rushed out. A look of shock was on his face when our eyes met. I was speechless. David grabbed my arm and said "Let's get out of here," so we ran to my car and drove off. Once we were a good five blocks away from his house, I noticed that David's lower lip was bleeding. I didn't have to ask him how it happened.

Although we had never talked about his father's abusive behavior, I had always suspected that something was off. But seeing that he couldn't hide what happened, David revealed the true nature of their father-and-son relationship. I felt very bad for him, but David refused my sympathy. It was very hard for him to tell me about what had happened, and he swore me to secrecy. He also told me to promise to never talk about the incident again.

As time went on, David became more and more withdrawn. He stopped wanting to hang out, and didn't enjoy doing the things we used to do. He also began losing weight. When I asked him if he was OK, he would always respond defensively and change the subject. I knew something was wrong, but what could I do about it?

Finally, a time came when everything I'd ever been taught, everything I knew to be true, was screaming at me to act. One night, while we were at my house playing video games, David asked me if I had ever thought about committing suicide. Although I had never pondered the issue, I knew David was reaching out for my help. At the time, David hated me for referring him to his school's counselor, just as I'd sensed he would. But that didn't stop me from trying to maintain our friendship.

David was referred to a psychologist and eventually returned to his former self. He wasn't necessarily what you'd call happy, but he had gained some weight and resumed some of his after-school activities. He even forgave me for telling on him. Although we lost touch and I don't know if David has had any bouts with depression since the last time we met, I believe that seeing a professional counselor was the only solution to his problem.

The essays in this chapter all reflect the gloom and despair that are often described as growing pains or teen angst. Most people don't feel that teenage boys have enough maturity to experience real depression, but the high rate of teenage suicide should remind us of just how serious and life-altering depression can be for adolescent boys.

Richard Ford's poem on depression is interesting for two reasons. He explains that he must hide his depression from people because he fears that they will not understand him. Many boys feel depression is a sign of weakness, and most choose to hide their true feelings so as not to come off negatively to their friends and family. The second point Richard brings up is his inability to ask for help. Because he is scared to admit to being depressed, he feels that there is no solution to his problem.

Sometimes there is one distinct cause for depression, but in Dolan Williams's narrative about his own battle with the dark side, he reveals all the various circumstances that can contribute to a boy's depression. Living on the outskirts of town fifteen miles away from school, Dolan must ride the bus to school while his friends drive past him in expensive cars. Disagreements with his mother, a lack of time for sports, and an inability to find a date as an African American in a predominately white school also exacerbate his gloomy outlook on life. In this essay, we see a young man struggling to overcome his background. I hope that someday Dolan will look back on his high school experience and smile.

While none of the letters included in this chapter depict boys taking their depression one step further, it is clear that depression can lead to a whole host of problems, including violent behavior, criminal activity, and even suicide. In Dan Fitzgerald's poem "Sleep Tight" the writer addresses the issue of runaways. The boy in the poem feels obligated to leave home and spare his mother from having to watch her son go through so much pain. He feels incapable of solving his emotional problems, and decides to run away for the good of his family.

> **Richard Ford,** 17, Palo Alto, California

I FEEL SO DAMN DEPRESSED

From all the school and all the work I feel so stressed
From all the people I'm around I feel so depressed
From God I know I'm blessed
But I still feel down
And I get more depressed when I see joy all around
I wish that was me smiling but I still have frown
No matter what I do can't turn it around
No money or car can soothe the pain that's in me
I'm so damn depressed but I still remain friendly
People think that I'm happy but I know it's not true
I feel so down and depressed and I feel so blue
Feeling this way is the thing that I rue
I try all my hardest but there's nothing I can do
Some say I dwell in the past but it's hard not to
I feel so down and depressed and I feel so blue

> **Dolan Williams,** 17, Phoenix, Arizona

Unfortunately, most people don't think that guys get depressed. And that's saddening. The reason for that may be because we mask so well. Most girls tend to wear their heart on their sleeve, so you can usually tell if they're depressed. Guys, on the other hand have their feelings sealed in a wooden box in a bomb shelter just north of New Guinea!

I tend to feel depressed every now and then. I've never actually told anybody about it because I fear that they'll think my reasons for depression are really trivial and make fun of me.

I've been going to predominantly white schools my entire life so I've made plenty of white friends, but even though I'm familiar with how white people act, I still feel like an outsider occasionally. Most everybody I know is like, "Dolan, I wish I were a big black guy like you." But it's not all it's cracked up to be, trust me. People tend to make unfair assumptions about you without even getting to know you. Some people automatically assume I know how to dance, or listen to rap, or know all the gang signs. I can't dance, I may listen to rap, but I've also got some Limp Bizkit and Korn in my collection too, and I've never ever been affiliated with a gang of any kind and I don't feel knowing gang signs is a knowledge that comes with birth in black people.

Meeting girls while I'm with my friends is hard too. When my friends and I go to meet girls or something, the girls are automatically interested in the white guys and the big black guy is kind of left behind for the moment. It's practically impossible to find a girl here where black people make up only 4 percent of the entire population of nearly 20 million in the state. So the whole time while everybody I know has found somebody, I'm left with nobody, and it's usually because I'm a different race, which is retarded. And that depresses me.

And, just like at any school, there are the haves, and the have-nots. A lot of my friends are definitely the haves with their nice cars and big homes. I, on the other hand, am a have-not. The fact that I have so little is definitely a major factor in most of my depression.

Also, some of my depression is due to the fact that I envy my friends too much. All the time I hear them talking about how they're going to their cabin up in Flagstaff, Arizona, or how their parents gave them two thousand dollars to detail their new car. Or when I was talking to some of my senior friends my sophmore year they would say, "Oh, I didn't get any scholarships to college, but my parents can afford it." It never bothered me until lately and now I finally see how little my family has. And that's what depresses me the most. I hate being broke, but the worst part about it, to me, is I can't really relate to and talk to any of my friends about it. They really don't have any idea how much money we *don't* have. Not a single one of my close friends has to go through what I go through every day. They don't know how lucky they are to have a car of their own that Mommy and Daddy pay for, and to not have to return to a messy, cramped home every day and have your mom take all of her frustrations from a job she hates out on you because you're close by.

My freshman year in high school is when I first started battling with depression. We found out that year that my mother had diabetes. This put a strain on everybody in the family and I had to take on quite a few more responsibilities, such as staying home on the weekends to baby-sit my sister. My grades started to slip a little and that didn't help a bit.

Sophmore year was when the depression started coming on a little harder. That was about the first time that I realized that we were broke. My entire life I had believed that when I was sixteen I was going to get a car to drive to and from school. And I didn't care what kind of car it was. As long as it was an automatic and had air-conditioning. Yeah, right. But not getting a car didn't bother me as much as I thought it would because, of course, my mom was going to pay for my insurance on her car, right? Sweet dreams. I was still stuck depending on Phoenix's horrible public transit system. You see, I live about fifteen miles away from where I go to school. That translates into a one-and-a-half-hour bus ride, in the heat, five days a week. Now, to most people this wouldn't sound so bad, but I've been doing it for the past ten years. I have the wonderful opportunity to wait twenty, thirty minutes for a warm, late bus to stroll by, only to have the driver deny me access because "there are already too many people."

As I walked to the bus stop every day after school to prepare for my road trip, I would always see my friends drive by and honk their horns and wave. I wished they would have asked me if I would like a ride home every once in a while but that hardly ever happened. I tried my hardest not to ask my friends for a ride because I had begun to notice that whenever I did, they would have this weird "Daaaammmnn!" look on their face. And since everybody else was driving except for me, I had to decline if they asked me to go anywhere at the spur of the moment because I never had (and still don't) any money. A lot of times I just wanted to transfer out of my school and go to a school where there were more people like me and I wouldn't feel so much like an outcast.

That was also the same year I began to drink. I told my friends that I started drinking because I was tired of looking like a doofus at parties, but the real reason was because I wanted to drink my penniless sorrows away.

Junior year has been the toughest by far. My downward spiral started the very first day of school in the '99–'00 school year. At 6:30 that morning I and the rest of the varsity football team had to run a mile along a canal that stretches across a park that's just behind our school. I obviously hadn't prepared hard enough for the season and finished with a time of 13:01. I went through my first day without a hitch. After school we had practice at around 6:00. We worked hard and I almost passed out and threw up. I didn't get any of my homework done until 1:30 that morning and had to wake up again at 5:00 the next morning to go lift.

After that second morning I decided that I wouldn't be able to play football this year. Sleep just couldn't compete with playing football 90 percent of my day and trying to make a 4.0 GPA so I can earn a scholarship. I went to my football coach the next afternoon and told him the bad news. I also went to my basketball coach and told him that I wouldn't be able to play basketball either because of the same reasons. That had really sent me into a small depression too because sports has always been a part of my life. Every single year ever since I was five years old I have been playing a sport or several sports at once, and not playing football and basketball weighed very heavily upon me. I was finally going to be able to play on a really good football team for once with all the returning starters being seniors, and I was one of only five juniors to be selected on a team of nearly forty-five people, and that would kind of thrust me into the spotlight a little and I liked that. But that wasn't going to happen. That was another thing that depressed me, a lot.

I had also been fighting with my mom a whole bunch. We had it out seven days a week and that really got me down. I don't like fighting with people and especially with my mom because she knows exactly how to make it hurt the most. She has a bad habit of insulting me all of the time and I have a bad habit of talking back, which she really doesn't like. She made me feel really stupid a lot of times and it began to shatter my self-confidence quite a bit and I wasn't going to let her do that, so one night in late '99, I decided to run away from home once and for all. She had gone to take my brother home that night and just before that she had insulted me in one way or another and she made me cry. I was like, "this is bullshit. I'm not going to let her make me cry. I'm leaving."

I packed up my stuff for school the next day and put on my

hat, my Payless sandals, and my CD player and I was gone. I
had no idea where I was going after I left my mom my note. I
thought maybe I'd just sleep in a parking lot or find a shelter
or a park or even a bus stop or something. I didn't know. I
eventually decided that I'd go to my friend's house for the
night. The only problem was that he lived just two minutes
from school, which was, of course, fifteen miles away. Oh well.
I'm not going to punk out and let my mom win this battle. I
walked and walked and walked and eventually made it to my
friend's driveway. And that's as far as I went. I couldn't force
myself to knock on their door at 1:00 A.M. I was so afraid that
they were going to turn me away or have a look of disgust on
their face that I just sat out by their recycling bin with my shirt
off staring at the stars.

I finally caved in and walked down to the local convenience
store, called my mom, and asked her to give me a ride home.
I felt horrible doing it and I really didn't want to at all but I
felt I had no other options at this time of night. I never told
my friend about it either. I just wanted the things to go away.

The entire fiasco sent me into a deep depression that lasted
nearly a month. Every day after school I would just come home
and go to sleep. I lost all drive to do anything. I stopped doing
my homework. I stopped studying. I gave up on trying to get
with any of the girls at school. I started drinking more. I just
kind of shut myself off from the world for seven days a week.
I didn't even feel like talking to anybody, laughing, watching
television, socializing with anybody, or going to school. I began
to ditch school a lot more than I ever had before, and I really
didn't care. I lost all drive to want to learn anything at all. I
was watching a commercial, which asked parents if their kids
were showing these signs of depression, and I fit every single
one of them.

Since I've told no one about my illness, just being able to
write about it has helped out tremendously. I'm hoping and
looking for ways to get over my depression. I've been taking

small steps in overcoming it and, thankfully, they seem to be working.

> **Dan Fitzgerald,** 17, Valhalla, New York

SLEEP TIGHT

Mother, Mommy, Mommy Dearest,
You will not believe this,
But I'm leaving town,
This afternoon.

There was nothing on the radio,
When I was watching "Jerry's Show,"
But I've gone away.
And I won't be back today.

Dinner comes and dinner goes,
But the story no one knows
Is the pain I had to live with.

It is not your fault at all,
You had done nothing wrong,
And I don't wanna hear you cry tonight,
Baby sleep tight.

No one has
Seen the light,
As I had,
In your eyes.

And the rain
Washed away,
All the pain
I had inside.

13

Between Worlds

"WHAT ARE YOU?" People have always asked me about my ethnic background, so I'd had plenty of opportunity to come up with a pat response.

"What do you think I am?"

Common guesses ranged from Italian, Greek, Turkish, Arabic, or just plain Middle Eastern. The truth is my parents are both from Iran. I, however, was born in New York City. Although there weren't many other Iranians living in my town or going to my school, I never felt any different from anyone else.

My classmates hardly ever judged me on the basis of my cultural background. Despite the fact that I was one of only two students of Iranian descent in my high school, I always felt accepted by my peers and their parents. Although I didn't think this unusual at the time, I now attribute this lack of prejudice to the open-minded and highly educated population that made up the community. The fact that I grew up in a suburb of New York City, probably the most ethnically diverse city in the country, must have had an impact on the way I was treated as well.

Given the progressive attitudes of my hometown, I was completely sheltered from the reality of discrimination elsewhere. This fact hit me like a ton of bricks during my freshman year in college. Like most college boys out on their own for the first time, I wanted to make new friends and meet girls. Joining a fraternity promised to fulfill both these wishes. Listening to the reports of the various fraternities' coolness quotients, I finally settled on joining a house with one of the best reputations.

Everything was going fine. I'd gotten in without a problem and found the house's rep to be well deserved. The whole process was so simple that I would never have thought to write about it if it hadn't been for the rumors that began to circulate a few weeks into the first semester.

Word had it that some of the older brothers had been insulting the new pledges for their ethnicity. Hearing talk of racial slurs, I suddenly felt as if I was a stranger in a strange world. Although I had heard about racism and discrimination many times, it had never hit so close to home. I tried to attribute the closed-minded behavior of some of the brothers to the fact that my school was situated in the Midwest and many of the school's students came from small towns with little or no diversity.

Hard as I tried, my best attempts to ignore the problem were futile. The situation was getting worse with every passing day. I could feel the animosity that my ethnicity inspired, and could no longer avoid the confrontations that my unusual last name provoked. The prejudice was shocking, eye-opening, and most of all, profoundly disturbing. In fact, I have a hard time talking about it to this day.

To make a long story short, I (along with four other minority pledges) wound up reevaluating my options and choosing a fraternity better suited to my particular needs. When I first pledged the house that I would later become very fond of, I realized that it was a lot more sophisticated than the fraternity I'd first joined. Many of the guys came from large cities or suburbs just like my own. I was finally at home.

Suffice it to say, my college experience turned out to be the happiest time of my life. Through my fraternity, I made many good friends with whom I still remain close to this very day. But for all the fun I had in college, I still looked forward to going home to New York during school breaks. I now know why I will always feel comfortable in the confines of this great big city, and will never take the open-mindedness of my hometown for granted again.

For the minorities and immigrant boys whose pieces are included in this chapter, cultural difference is the most important issue of their lives, an issue that informs everything they do from dating to academics to friendships. Whether it's an immigrant who is trying to learn the English language or a young minority student trying to fit in, all of these stories can teach us something about the many struggles that being different presents for young boys.

"My Greatest Challenge," by Vinh Do, addresses a host of issues particular to young immigrant boys. Brought up in two different worlds, Vinh finds himself in the precarious position of trying to lay down a new foundation as an American citizen. But assimilating to his new surroundings creates a myriad of difficulties that Vinh describes in painfully explicit detail.

While Clayton Lee's personal essay touches on the same subject as "My Greatest Challenge," it is ultimately about the more positive aspects of being an immigrant. Forced to rely on himself for everything, the author acquires a pride in his heritage, a strong character, and a boundless determination to succeed.

Justin Lock's poem "Courting the Farmer's Daughter" focuses on the issue of interracial dating. Meeting his girlfriend's family for the first time, the writer tries to fit in, only to find himself confronted with social and cultural differences at every turn. Although the "farmer's daughter" herself is not hung up on the issue of race, her family's prejudice, born of the "farmer's" frightful experience in Vietnam, makes Justin uncomfortable about his Asian heritage.

Finally, "My Native Warrior," by Mikela Jones, is a heartfelt and passionate ode to the role models and leaders of the past. Living on a modern Indian reservation, he finds himself in a precarious bind. Although he has a lot of pride in his cultural legacy, he is deeply disconcerted by the lack of role models in his life. Living day to day without anyone to guide him, Mikela must rely on himself to preserve the community bonds that give him as much strength as they do a sense of identity and belonging.

> **Vinh Do,** 17, Santa Ana, California

MY GREATEST CHALLENGE

The tired passengers of the Boeng 747 arrived at Los Angeles airport on November 31, 1995. It was a cold night when I first put my hopeful steps on the U.S. soil. I was overwhelmed with everything I saw, including those figures with blond hair and blue eyes. Suddenly I felt lost and bewildered. Fears arose in my mind. Those fears were the enemies that I would have to face for the next four years.

At first, the air was different, and the food no longer delicious. Later on, I kind of got used to it. My family and I moved to an apartment with a big sign on the door that read, "Rental." We lived in the area called Little Saigon. It was an average-sized community made up mostly of Vietnamese. Everyone spoke Vietnamese and I did not have the chance to practice my English, which was both an advantage and a disadvantage.

Because the apartment was cheap and there was no heater, I spent most of my mornings sitting out in the sun to get warm. Once, my uncle called me up and said, "People will call the cops if you keep sitting out on the street. They will think that you are looking at their houses." His words really scared me. I never again dared to sit on the street.

I enrolled in McGarvin Intermediate School. Entering as an eighth grader was not my wish, but it was my destiny. The most difficult part was the language. I was unable to comprehend it. The bell rang and first period began. My E.L.D. teacher was a Chinese lady with curly hair and an unattractive face. When I listened to what she said, I felt like I was listening to the language of the Native Americans. I had taken a few English courses back in my country, but somehow I could not get the drift of what my teacher said. My friends often had to translate her instructions for me. I was very fortunate because most of the E.L.D. students in my class spoke my language, Vietnamese.

My first year in the United States was horrible. It was something that I will never forget.

Going to school with the usual clothes that I wore back in my country was no longer a fashion in the United States. In fact my clothes were considered the "geeks" type. Kids wore pants that were as wide as my jacket. It was later that I realized those pants were cool.

Most of the clothes I got were from charities, garage sales, and churches. As a result, they were a few inches shorter than they needed to be. Every time I sat down, the pants showed two inches of my bare calves. In class, I sometimes had to kneel down to stretch my pants to make them look longer.

My old shoes had worn away, so I asked my dad to buy me a new pair of shoes. I was ecstatic to wear the new shoes to school. My friends were very nice. They did not make any negative comments about my shoes. Not everyone was so kind. I remember that one student, whom I did not know, publicly announced that the shoes I was wearing were women's shoes. To my great confusion, I could not make out the difference between women's shoes and men's shoes. When I got home, I told my parents the whole thing, but they could not afford to buy me another pair of tennis shoes because of financial difficulties. I don't blame them.

Later I found out that there was a little pink line on the
shoes that made them woman's shoes. I used the pen to shade
the pink line to make it black. I had to wear them for the rest
of the school year. This took away all of my confidence, as I
realized that what you wear can affect how you feel inside.

My biggest challenge was at La Quinta High School when I
was a freshman. Trying to adapt to the new environment was
my only goal. I was really, really scared when anyone came up
to me and spoke what they called English. Still I was able to
hold on to a couple of friends that spoke my language. I understood a little bit of English by then. One day, when my
friends and I were talking, a girl came up to me and said, "One
of my friends likes you. Why don't you go and check her out?"

I smiled nervously and foolishly followed her. To my great
embarrassment, those girls were laughing at me and said something that I could not understand. Suddenly I realized that the
whole thing was a joke. What could I do? I obviously could not
disappear from the face of the earth, nor could I cry. I was a
man; therefore, I kept my pride.

After a few years, I could speak and write some English, but
not as well as the others, of course. I could never be like them.
My accent had become quite a joke to everyone in my class. I
felt humiliated, but it was my God-given voice and there was
nothing I could do about it. My haircut had made the best
comedy show ever to some students; however, the mature ones
remained quiet, knowing when to keep their mouths shut.

My biggest confusion was the word "cool." What is cool?
Why does everyone I know want to be cool? According to the
dictionary, cool is calmly bold or impudent. What it really
means is wearing clothing or acting in a manner that resembles
gang styles, a famous rock group, or a famous person. If one
wanted to be considered cool, all he had to do was shave his
head, wear baggy clothes, and start a fight in school. Are those

things cool? According to most students, those things are cool. Then I wondered why would people want to be cool if it meant doing those things. These were the things that I saw every day in school.

By now, life had settled down. My family's income became pretty steady; I managed to get a haircut just like everyone else; and I dressed just like everyone else. What I was trying to do was what they called a "melting pot." I was trying to be one of them.

Time slowly faded in the mist of my unhappiness. One more year passed unnoticed in my consciousness. On a cozy morning in one of my classes, I decided it was time to notice some girls. I stared at this one particularly pretty girl. She was not so far away that I couldn't overhear her conversation:

She said, "That stupid guy over there is staring at me."

Her friend snapped, "I think he likes you."

The girl made an ugly face and replied, "Ewwww."

I was crestfallen, not because she didn't like me, but because my self-esteem had been badly damaged ever since the first day of school. After all these years of trying to blend into their environment, I was still different.

It was then that I learned how to survive these terrible ordeals. I learned not to care what people think or say about me. I learned not to expect anything from anyone. In a way, they completely changed my personality. Perhaps these experiences sharpened me. They changed me from a young, shy, sensitive boy into a whole new person. In a way, they completely changed my personality. The smile on my face ceased to exist. Suddenly I saw everyone as my enemies. I disliked everyone in school, except a couple friends of mine. I learned to live alone with my thoughts and my feelings.

Still, I know that there are always possibilities to do something or to become someone. Life can be a wonderful experience or it can be a terrible ordeal depending on how I live it. I am beginning to see that now. One should take advantage of the opportunities this country has to offer, and I am doing just that.

▶ Clayton Lee, 18, Ukiah, California

Many factors have gone into the creation of the person my mom chose to name Lee Kung-Yung, or Clayton. My early memories sometimes seem to escape my simple mind, but I have preserved a few mental photographs of my life as a child. I remember many smoky plane rides as my family traveled from Taiwan to my birthplace of San José, Costa Rica, and back again. There are also the pictures that I let collect dust for I would rather recall the many adventurous trips to amusement parks, and the images of my arrival to a new, mysterious land, feeling just like Columbus.

Growing up around a Spanish baby-sitter while my parents worked to make a living as restaurant owners, I was bombarded by the Chinese, Spanish, and English languages. Finally, we settled down in a small, rural town where I was Americanized and taken over by a new culture and environment. Like my mother and father, I too struggled to find a niche in this society.

I began my journey as a student ambitiously, learning to appreciate the American life and language, while at the same time trying not to lose touch with my ethnicity and cultural roots. In this predominantly Caucasian town, remaining an individual and representing my culture proved a formidable challenge. I faced much belittling, American boys pulling their eyes back, mocking the beautiful and intricate language of my people.

My parents' situation was no less difficult. My mother worked as hard as she could to adapt to this new way of living, while my dad scornfully criticized the American ways and found security in a world where he was the essence of supreme knowledge and wisdom. As I began to grow accustomed to recess, playing, and all the other things that kids do, my mom was having a harder time dealing with my father's verbal abuse, his painful tormenting of my older brother, and his pride that would not let him be wrong.

At the tender age of eight, I saw my parents get divorced. My father moved to San Francisco to be as close to his native culture as possible, while my mother became a single parent. I soon conformed to the monthly visits with my father, still trying to be something he could not, and the absence of alimony checks. I had to learn to tell my curious American friends of my single-parent household while hiding my family's financial status.

As the years progressed, my father's visits grew shorter and less frequent. Each time he would come he preached the same thing: "Get into a university. You don't want to be a kitchen hand, do you?" I knew he wanted me to be something, but I soon realized I wanted to be something, too. I did not want to follow the same path he had, living off the government in a one-room flat and criticizing everything around him with a negative mentality.

Living without the glamour of father/son activities and a loving relationship has made me come to grips with myself. I now realize that it has made me bolder and more independent. I may not have had my dad at all the Little League games, but I had my passion, and the dedication to hit the ball as far as I could, run as fast as my scrawny legs would let me, and work as hard as I could to reach victory and happiness.

One event that helped me understand my Chinese roots was an enlightening trip to my native land of Taiwan. For one short month, I lived in my element. I indulged in the heritage and culture of my very existence, heretofore clouded by hot dogs, Hollywood, and the American way.

Accompanied by my older sister, I took advantage of this

voyage to dig up my cultural roots and plant newer, stronger seeds in the nurturing presence of my extended family. Each day I learned something that tickled my mind. I was hungry for more each time I skipped through the damp, cluttered alleyways between skyscraping apartment housings and corporate buildings, each time I scanned the busy highway networks from the highest floors of my aunt's apartment complex, and each time I maneuvered through the cluttered bodies gathered together on public transportation. I dreaded leaving and still recall the home cooking, the daily trends, and the overall beauty of the distinguished culture as I compare and contrast it to the society in which I live. To this day, this visit lives in my heart and drives my pride and perseverance.

>**Justin Lock,** 18, Highland Park, Illinois

COURTING THE FARMER'S DAUGHTER

I remember the first time I
Spent the night at a girl's house
I crossed three hours of cornfields
And a world of soybeans
In a Greyhound bus
Just to get there

I remember walking through the
back door
it was June
and hot as hell

her family was watching *Wheel of Fortune*
they made her watch too
I remember the flag

Nailed across the wall in the living room
Just like the one in front of the post office
But this one not moving

I remember the country ribs and corn on the cob
I had never imagined eating something so big
I remember somebody, her uncle, going out for beer
and ice
to beat the heat

it rained that night
but even that didn't help much
the drops falling like hot tears

I remember we snuck off after supper
to the milo field across town

she held my hand and tried to explain
that her father had fought in Nam
and that he has hated yellow boys ever since
they tried to kill him in jungle

she cried as she apologized
scalding water beating down the crop
and as the rain splattered my shirt
I silently prayed
for the downpour to wash me of my
color

> **Mikela Jones,** 18, Redwood Valley, California

MY NATIVE WARRIOR

My Native Warrior, where have you gone
I need you to teach me what's right and what's wrong.
The only warrior I know is the one of the past,
You changed so quick, and so fast.

Once you wore moccasins, buckskin, and beads
But now in this lifestyle they are no longer necessities or
    needs.
You used to wear that feather in your hair; big, strong, and
    bright.
Now it is gone, it's out of sight.

But I know it is now held in the heart and in no other place.
I miss the proud cries and the war paint upon your face.
I walk on this planet like a ghost
Lost, scared, confused.
Awaiting my vision that I need most.

Warrior, I cry, what is it?
Is it you or is it me, is it he or is it she?
I want it to be me! I want it to be me!
My Native Warrior, where have you gone?
I need you, I need you, I am all alone.

You are in the deep sleep like our brother the bear.
You need to wake up and be aware,
Aware of what we need, what we lost and what is on the way.
You used to lead us day to day.

You abandoned your brothers, sisters, and wives.
You totally forgot about our lives.

I know you're asleep and you will awake,
I know that you will realize it was just a mistake.

Until you awake from your rest,
The only thing I can do is my best.
My Native Warrior, where have you gone?
You have been asleep for too long.

I'm haunted by the dreams that keep me up late.
I'm full of fire, full of anger, and full of hate.
I'm full of love, full of happiness, and full of joy.
But I still am confused if I'm a man or just a boy.

You've fought battles for your people and you won.
How you gonna forget me, I'm your son.
I need you, I need the ceremonies and the song.
They've been away for too long.

So I look to the Creator and listen to the wind,
To show me where I must begin.
Begin to be proud, strong to be an Indian.
My Native Warrior where have you been?
My Native Warrior, we shall meet again.

Epilogue

AS I LOOKED over the selections included in this book one last time, an old adage kept popping into my head: "Boys will be boys." I had always heard people saying this, but could never figure out just what they meant. If they were trying to say that boys will always get into fights, have the emotional maturity of two-year-olds, and be incapable of sustaining relationships, well, then they were wrong. But if their words were meant to convey the fact that boys are hurting, crying out, trying to fit in, and dealing with a myriad of issues such as peer pressure, friendship, racial conflict, and violence, then they were right on—boys *will* be boys.

Through writing about my past and reading these poignant letters, many of which even brought a tear to my eye, I discovered that I am glad that boys will always be boys. I am glad that boys will always defy our expectations. I am glad that boys will always try to rise above their circumstances. I am glad that boys do stand up for themselves. I am glad that, if given the chance, boys will always speak out.

For a long time, I was silent about the trials and tribulations of my wonder years. I kept it all inside, and never thought that I would one day share my experiences with the world. To tell you the truth, I never considered my life important enough to document. After all, who was I? Just a young boy trying to find my way in the world. Along the journey to making this book a reality, I learned that I had something of value to contribute. I learned that all of us, we boys, have to be proud of who we are and never stop talking about the experiences that shape our lives, our future, and the world around us.

Having mailed more than five thousand letters to schools, I was relieved when I received over six hundred responses from boys all over the country. Although I swore to my editor that I had no doubts that boys would write in, I was not as confident as I let on. When the replies started coming in, I couldn't believe just how many boys were willing to put themselves on the line and speak candidly about everything from first love to violence. If the experience of reading these many poems, essays, and stories taught me anything, it's that there is something to be learned from every boy. Likewise, each of the letters in this book has something to teach us. All of them offer a glimpse into the well-hidden, but no less vital, emotional lives of teenage boys.

Of course, there are also those letters that can never be published. Despite my supplications and promises of strict anonymity, a few boys were either afraid or ashamed to share the thoughts they'd revealed to me with the outside world. One who'd written about his family worried lest he disturb his ailing father, another, who'd discussed school and popularity, feared that if his thoughts become public, he would no longer be safe in the hallways and locker rooms. Saddest of all were the circumstances of a boy who'd written about the lingering effects of his first heartbreak. Having read his son's rather sentimental submission, the writer's father flat out refused to let his son publish the touching work—anonymous or otherwise.

Thus, the letters in this book are only a small sample of the many voices that are daring us to listen and react. They are not written by strangers you have yet to meet. The boys in this book are your next-door neighbors, your best friends, your brothers, and your sons. While I couldn't include all of the

pieces I received due to the book's limited space, it is with great
humility that I extend my gratitude to all of the boys who participated in this project. I thank you for your honesty, your
generosity, your courage, and most important, for just being
boys.

About the Authors

Raised in Scarsdale, New York, JOHN NIKKAH earned his B.A. in psychology from the University of Illinois at Urbana-Champaign in 1996. There he served as an interfraternity peer counselor, and has since gone on to pursue a master's in psychology at the New School of Social Research in New York City. He will be receiving his master's degree in spring 2000, and is planning to pursue a Ph.D. in clinical psychology in the fall.

LEAH FURMAN lives and writes in New York City. She has written more than fifteen books.